ONLY MY LIFE

❖ A SURVIVOR'S STORY ❖

LOUIS DE WIJZE
as told to Kees van Cadsand

Translated by Victor de Wijze

Catawba Publishing Company

Only My Life: A Survivor's Story
By Louis de Wijze, as told to Kees van Cadsand
Translated by Victor de Wijze

Cover Design by Cara Johnston
Cover Photo by Ted Axelrod

ISBN number: 1-59712-027-8
2nd Edition

Printed in the United States of America by
Catawba Publishing Company
5945 Orr Rd., Suite F
Charlotte, NC 28213

www.catawbapublishing.com

*This book is for my wife,
children and grandchildren and
is also dedicated to little Piszta,
who was murdered at the end of
January 1945, somewhere between
Olomouc and Prague*

By Louis de Wijze

❖ THE SUBSTITUTE ❖

September 1944. It is one of those evenings, again. As our group arrives at the campsite, we can see them, dark and threatening against the evening sky. Two gallows this time, no doubt for as many convicted.

At the sound of some well-known march music played by the camp brass band, we walk toward the *appelplatz*, a courtyard where roll call is held, and take our places. I am standing in the second row from the front and will soon be forced to watch the spectacle from close by.

We see a prisoner, hands tied behind his back, being taken to the front. The music has stopped now, and immediately the tension envelops us in a chilly fog. I hear the fast, quivering breath of someone behind me. Then, the voice of the SS officer in charge, like the staccato of a Sten gun, resonates on the *appelplatz*. In the name of the fuhrer, we are told, two prisoners will be executed this evening.

Whatever "offense" has been committed, the gallows are ready; the sentence was never in doubt. I am looking at the poor fellow in front of us and see an emaciated human being with bluish skin. His gaze is no longer in our world. Only with a mere thread of breath does he still seem connected to us.

We hear that the convicted man was one of two people who attempted to escape. The other fugitive had, however, not been captured. But there will be two executions tonight no matter what, the officer shouts at us with a roaring voice. In retaliation, one of us will be picked on the spot to dangle on the second gallows. My location in the group is very dangerous, but it is too late to try surreptitiously to move to the back. Everything goes like lightning.

Three SS officers are walking past the rows to pick out a victim. I see the henchmen come closer. How should I look? How should I stand? Shall I look them in the eyes, or cast mine down?

Another four steps, three, two. The shiny boots suddenly stop less than ten feet from where I am. They want me. The thought pierces right through me! That very same moment, my life flashes by me. One, maybe two seconds, and I've disassociated myself from my surroundings.

A sudden noise brings me back to reality. A few yards to the left, a prisoner is punched and kicked out of the ranks to the front. Didn't he keep a straight face? Was he trembling? Was he too obviously trying to hide? It does not matter. The choice has been made; the substitute guilty one has been found. The cries and pleas of the poor man are suffocated by dull thuds. In no time, he is standing handcuffed next to the other. His body is shaking from top to bottom. I'm starting to feel a belated trembling in my own hands and knees. An icy chill rolls down my spine. I'm taking a few deep breaths.

It's over, I tell myself. Stay calm, don't move. Slowly, very slowly, I start to regain control over my limbs. The deadly fear is fading away. As if in a trance, both victims climb the scaffold. The second man is now completely apathetic. In deadly silence, the nooses are put on. A snarling command and the trap doors disappear. A short convulsion. "Hats off." Like robots, we take our hats off our bald heads, and at the sounds of the band, we march toward the gallows. By the time our group passes by, the bodies have already gone limp and lifeless.

A few yards away, two officers nonchalantly smoke cigarettes. They look relaxed and content, as if they have just been raking their yard.

By Louis de Wijze

❖ ALONG THE ABYSS ❖

Alongside the little train platform in transit camp Westerbork, in the Netherlands, I say good-bye to my sister, Kitty, and her husband, Leo. There is not much we can say. We hug each other for a long time and stare over each other's shoulders with watery eyes. "Be careful over there," Kitty whispers. "And if you see Father and Mother, please give them a big hug from me." The only thing I can do is nod. A few minutes later, the train, halting and screeching, starts to move. Through the vents at the top of our cattle car, we try to wave and call as long as we can in order to keep contact with those who stay behind. It is Tuesday, March 23, 1944. I am twenty-one years old.

Early that morning, around 4 A.M., we had been awakened. This time my name was one of those called for deportation to Poland. Feverishly, I had tried in the few remaining hours to be taken off the list, running all over the place to several authorities. To no avail. The entire Bauer Group, the labor group that I belonged to, was deported in retaliation for the escape of one of the prisoners. Our group consisted of young and strong men. We felt ourselves to be the best command group of the entire Westerbork camp. It was we who had to do the heavy and difficult jobs, both in and outside the camp. For instance, we had built the railroad between the camp and the Oranje Canal in a few weeks. Later on, via this waterway, the wreckage of downed planes was transported to the railroad and from there to the camp, where the metals were sorted and recycled for the war industry.

Because of reasonably good food in the camp and tough, manual labor, we gradually got into excellent physical condition. For a long time we fooled ourselves into thinking that our group had become so in-dispensable that we would be spared deportation. Every week we had seen the trains leave Westerbork for camps in the east. We had seen old and sick people, pregnant women, toddlers and babies, and people on stretchers all being loaded into the trains. We didn't understand. What got into the Germans to take these people away? Of what use would they be in the camps in the east? "There are better hospitals over there," some said. Others heard that the elderly will be housed in special homes. But most of us, young people, were silent and put our uneasy feelings aside. As long as it wasn't your turn, life at Westerbork was bearable. But then another Tuesday came. The previous evening, the hated train had arrived at the camp. This time for the young and strong as well.

Mothers bitched at their children, and fathers shouted angrily for no apparent reason. A restless night followed. Many people stayed awake for the early-morning reading of the list with the names of the deportees. Relief and sorrow were intermingled that next morning, until the train, chock-full of people, left around noon.

That was the way my parents had left on February 16, 1943. "We are going with you," Kitty and I had said when we heard that our parents were on the list. "We're not going to let you leave by yourselves." But decidedly they had rejected us. "No, you both stay here. End of discussion." Together with our foster sister, Inge, they had boarded the train. The train doors had been latched, all very quietly, as if it were a commuter train. Camp Commander Gemmeker had smiled and walked alongside the train with his Alsatian. A shrieking whistle. A plume of smoke in the distance.

It is quiet in our railroad car. We are moving in synchronicity with the thudding and shaking train. Poland-the name had acquired an eerie ring to it back in Westerbork, but we have absolutely no idea what to expect. What do they want from us? Will we be put in an extremely hard labor camp, as we all expect? But what of the railroad car behind us with all the mentally retarded from the asylum? A vague but persistent fear stays with us the entire journey. A queasy feeling lingers in our stomachs. We hold on to one another.

Isn't our group the very best? There must be a reason that all of us have been put in one car, and not with the usual eighty to one car, but only fifty. Didn't we get a new septic barrel and new paper mattresses? That must be a special privilege for the Bauer Group.

Time goes by slowly. Through the air openings we can tell by the landscape and the names of villages that we have crossed the German border. We often stop for hours, for no apparent reason. On one of those occasions, the sliding door of our car is opened. Two young SS officers climb inside. Their ugly faces are etched in my memory: The first one has a flabby face with connecting eyebrows; he looks dumb and cruel. The other one has an expressionless, sheepish look. "Watches," they shout, and in no time we've lost our watches. If you protest, you get knocked down or floored. Less than an hour later, the train stops again, and a second search for watches is conducted. Eddie Silber, a hairdresser from our group, dares to tell these fine gentlemen that some of their colleagues have already done a similar search. To no avail. Everything of value-fountain pens, wallets, purses, a cigarette case-is shamelessly taken away from us. We receive a few more of these impromptu visits during that first day. Then the night sets in.

Only a few of us manage to get some sleep. The uncomfortable cattle car and uneasiness are keeping us awake. Sometimes a high-pitched cry pierces the darkness. It is coming from the mentally ill who are completely up-set. Where are we now? Did I correctly hear "Berlin Span-dau" when we made a quick stop? Again, a piercing cry from the other car, almost like the howling of a wild animal. Those poor people are probably much worse off than we are. They are packed like sardines, unable to understand what's happening to them, incapable of taking care of themselves.

At the end of an endless night, the locomotive hisses its white cloud of steam in the gray morning air. Huffing and puffing, the train starts to move, and life returns to our car. Some of us play cards, others are staring quietly ahead. In a corner, I eat some of the sandwiches that Kitty so caringly made for me. When the sun gradually replaces the nightly chill in the car, people start to talk again. There's even some laughter here and there.

Our courage is coming back. We'll make it over there, we keep telling one another. It is probably going to be tougher than Westerbork, but we're young and strong. The Bauer Group has gone through a lot worse, we reassure ourselves. The cries of the mentally ill are diffused by the sound of the racing wheels. That is a blessing.

This second day also slowly passes by. The many hours just standing still are the worst. Those moments you can clearly hear the shouting and knocking of the mental patients. It makes us ill at ease and irritated. Can nobody tell them to be quiet? For the fourth or fifth time today, the train comes to a standstill. The brakes are making a shrieking noise. Walter Sanders, a distant cousin of mine, lifts me up so that I can look outside through the vent. We have reached a fairly large railroad yard.

"Breslau," I read out loud from a sign along the track. The train suddenly rocks back and forth, twice. To the left, at the end of the train, I can see what's causing it. "They're disconnecting the food car," I call out. I jump down. Worried, we discuss the situation.

In Westerbork they had prepared food and drink for the journey and put it in a separate car. So far, we had been able to satisfy our eating and drinking needs with little packages that we had brought ourselves, but everything is gone by now. And right at this time, the food car is taken off. What does that mean?

The queasy feeling returns with full force. But it's not just hunger. We squat silently on our mattresses. The darkness sets in quickly, and the cold makes us shiver. Through the grate, we can see that it's started to snow. An icy shriek from the car with the mentally ill tells us it's going to be a hard night.

❖ GHOSTS ❖

We are deep into our third morning when the train stops. We hear the opening of the sliding doors of the first cars. All tense, we look at one another as the noises come our way. Then our door flies open. "Everybody out. All your luggage on the platform. Quick. Quick."

We grab our stuff, jump outside, and immediately find ourselves in a raging storm. Men in striped clothes hastily drive everybody off the train. The SS, their Alsatians on the leash, club any prisoners still holding on to their possessions. Right in front of us, the mentally ill are stumbling onto the platform, utterly filthy and bewildered. An unbearable stench emanates from their car. Some of them are carried, wrapped in horse blankets, and thrown on a waiting truck. With a lot of shouting, others are chased out right behind them.

Instinctively I hide in the crowd and quickly look for my friends of the Bauer Group. Silently, we huddle together. Orders are given for us to start walking. Stooped and timid, we move in the indicated direction. Next to the tracks I see a small, low railway building. Left and right there are numerous rows of big barracks.

The camp that we just arrived at must be huge, with tens of thousands of inhabitants. Ghostlike figures in striped clothes, identical to the ones who chased us off the train, walk in between the barracks. Way ahead of us is the truck with the mentally ill. A bluish-white thread of smoke curls from the exhaust pipe and evaporates immediately in the cold winter air.

After a fifteen- or twenty-minute walk, we arrive at a large building at the back of the camp. Hastily, we are driven inside. The mentally ill have already arrived and anxiously huddle together. Some of them are frothing at the mouth; their eyes are shooting from left to right. Others, in a demonic ecstasy, are endlessly swaying back and forth, back and forth.

The space we're in is the size of a big gym. When the last prisoners have been pushed inside, the doors are locked. Two armed SS officers position themselves at both doorposts. We wait a long, long time, becoming more nervous as time passes. Children start to cry; some of the mental patients shout loudly. Finally, an officer with a transport list in his hand arrives.

Roll call. That means counting. Everything has to be right. All names are called, including those of the mental patients. It is complete chaos as the mentally ill start to parrot each name. They are laughing and shouting, booing and grimacing. The SS officer no longer has any control over the situation but continues to rant and rave. When I finally hear the biting voice shout my name, I do not realize that this, for some time to come, is the last time I will be referred to as a human being.

"De Wijze, Louis."

"Here."

After repeated head counts, the numbers finally appear to add up. We slowly shuffle toward a big open door where two other officers divide the prisoners into two groups. Closer now, I see that almost all old people, children, and women are being directed to the right, the others to the left. Behind me, I hear the ranting and raving of the mental patients. They are probably kept apart, I still think in my innocence.

Suddenly, I am eye to eye with an SS officer. He looks me over. I quickly tell him in my best German, "I am twenty-one and would like to work." His gloved hand points to the left. As we are pushed and shoved forward- *"Schnell! Schnell"*- see a wall with arched iron doors to

By Louis de Wijze

my right, just like a bread oven. The fire is still smoldering. To my great joy, I soon notice that the entire Bauer Group has stayed together. But we don't get much time to realize what's happening to us.

Again, we are herded together. Now it's our turn to be loaded on the trucks. The growling vehicles are shaking us violently as they drive us to an unknown destination. What do they have in store for us? Are we going back to the train, or are we, maybe, being taken out of the camp? We soon realize that we must have left the camp because the trucks have been driving many minutes now. "Perhaps we'll have to work on a farm," one of the young men in our group suggests. But nobody reacts; the events after our arrival have paralyzed us. Everything seems like a dream, and we form no part of it. After another ten minutes, we arrive at our destination. Only the next morning do we learn that we are at Auschwitz, a camp with the slogan *"Arbeit machtfrei"* over the entrance gate.

It is nearly dark when we jump off the trucks. An icy wind pushes the snow underneath our clothes as we march along the street between the gray barracks, in rows of five. At building number 26, we are commanded to halt. Motionless, we wait. The snowstorm cuts us like a knife. Then suddenly: "Undress!" Undress? Aghast, we look at one another. Undress here, outside? But the first blows have already been dealt. "Move it, move it, faster, you filthy Jews." Quickly we undress, and in no time we are standing nude on the street. While undressing, I've managed to rip up my green napa leather riding pants. "They won't get these," I silently say to myself.

Shivering and stomping our feet against the biting cold, we stand there as minute after minute goes by. We are desperately trying to fend off the freezing snowstorm by jumping up and down and slamming our arms back and forth. Behind the windows of the building next to 26, heads, thin and shorn, look at us curiously but without any excitement. For over an hour we are exposed to the wintry cold. The Germans are not in a hurry and seem to ignore us all that time. They finally chase us inside, more dead than alive.

A number of prisoners are waiting to remove all the hair from our heads and bodies. It's a pretty rough procedure: They "plow" their hair clippers at dazzling speed over our heads. With dull razor blades-no soap is used-they tear away our body hair. All of a sudden, next to me, Eddie Sil-ber pokes me lightly in the ribs. Surreptitiously, he shows me his hands. In utter amazement I see that he's managed to smuggle his razor blade, soap, and brush inside. We quickly lather ourselves at the sink and shave off our body hair at the speed of lightning as best we can. Right after that, the clippers shave our heads, and harshly we are chased to another area.

Other prisoners are waiting to tattoo a number onto our left arms with what looks like a crown pen. They accomplish this in no time, and we are pushed and shoved again.

I look at my arm and see that, from now on, I'm number 175564. Not all six digits are equally perfect. The second number 5, maybe because of the crazy speed at which it was applied, is a little tattered. A few blue dots are missing. There is no time to think about my new "name." We rush on.

Our bloody bodies are disinfected with Lysol. They use rough burlap sacks to rub it on, and it stings like hell. But we just go on, up the stairs to the floor where a mountain of prison clothes are piled up. We grab a hat, pants, coat, flannel underpants, shirt, and socks and hurry to the spot where the shoes are. Feverishly, I look for a left and right clog. I'm lucky. Just before we are chased away again, I find a pair that reasonably fits me.

Shortly after, completely exhausted and dazed, I stand in the line-up in my blue-gray striped uniform in front of Block 26. Totally upset, we look at one another. It is hard to recognize us. Not a hint remains of those who just jumped off the trucks. Our strength and self-assurance have been replaced by a sense of deep humiliation. In one fell swoop everything has been taken from us. We're only numbers, statistics. Just like everyone else in this horrible place, we've become ghosts, shadows of ourselves.

Nauseated and confused, I am taken away with a small group to our new accommodations, Block 11. One hour later, we lie on the ice-cold concrete floor of the upper story, without any protection. Just before that, we received some bread and muddy coffee, the first and only food of this day.

Around me I hear some soft weeping. In our total loneliness, we endure the memories of the horrors of the previous day. It's starting to overpower me, too. Like in a dream, I see my parents in front of me, ready to leave Westerbork for their voyage to the east. It seems like an eternity. Now, I'm pretty sure I'll never see them again.

❖ IN QUARANTINE ❖

The next morning, shivering and chilled to the bone, we are rudely woken up. Stiff as a plank, I join the line that leads to the sinks in the washroom. All night we lay belly to back to try and keep our bodies warm. No blankets, no mattresses, no pillows, no heating. Our bed was a bare concrete floor.

Yesterday's weather has caused some of us to become gravely ill. Some are running a high fever. Surprisingly, I'm feeling reasonably fit and seem to have withstood yesterday's hardship without any noticeable ill effects. However, sick or not, in no time, everybody is assembled at the court-yard between Blocks 10 and 11, and the umpteenth head count since we've left Westerbork takes place.

With an obsession bordering on lunacy, the Germans count, recount, and count again. Everything has to be correct, has to be captured in numbers and quantities. We are no more than general cargo, samples without value, replaceable.

While we are standing there in the pale morning light, I'm looking past the backs of the other prisoners toward the basement below our block. Something is moving. Behind the window bars, I see thin, pale faces with hollow, feverishly glistening eyes. When I look more closely, I see that the cells of these living shadows are so small and low that the people in them can only squat. What kind of people are they? Why are they being kept like animals in cages far too small for them? I'm shivering in horror. In what kind of hellhole are we here? Can we expect the same fate as these poor people?

The minutes pass by, fifteen, thirty, sixty. Finally, a young, cleanly shaven SS officer appears in front of our group. He glances briefly at us with contempt. Then he opens his mouth, and in a biting tirade he shouts that we are now in main camp Auschwitz, a camp that in no way is a health resort. Breaking the camp rules and regulations will be severely punished. For the time being, we will have to stay in our block until further notice. That's all. No explanation.

Our guards still don't seem to be in any hurry. Flanked by their Alsatians, they chat with one another. The chill creeps up our legs and paralyzes our muscles. Next to me, someone's teeth chatter with the cold. He has a high fever. "I can't take it anymore," he whispers in a quivering voice. But he has to; he has no choice.

The icy wind takes our breath away. Our strength dissipates from our bodies. How much longer? In my mind, I'm starting to count to one hundred. It should be over by the time I reach that number. But my ritual doesn't seem to affect reality. Minute after minute goes by without anything happening.

Then, after an eternity, finally the order to go back inside. At that very moment, in front of the windows of Block 10, I see the pale, shorn heads of women. They are apathetically observing the events in the courtyard. I know those looks. They are similar to the ones that confronted us yesterday, when we were all naked in the snowstorm at Block 26. They are in the eyes of people who have seen it all before, experienced it all before. At the same time, they radiate an intense pity and sadness.

One of the guards notices that we have an audience. Ranting and raving, he runs to the window and quickly closes the shutters. I better hurry, because our guards have made it abundantly clear that they will kick anyone who hesitates, even for a moment, to follow their orders.

Back in the building, on the upper story, the sick finally are able to slide onto the concrete floor. They are exhausted. A young compatriot of mine, who appears to be from my former hometown, Boxmeer, a chemist by profession, squats next to them, puts his ear on their chests, listens, and taps. He concludes that some of them have contracted pneumonia.

A few hours later, the very ill are picked up and taken to the sick bay. We never see them again. The day goes by slowly.

Only now I realize that many members of the Bauer Group must have stayed behind at the big camp yesterday. I didn't see them in our block or at the roll call. Long after darkness has set in, we're huddling together again. The second night on the concrete floor is again an ice-cold agony.

The following morning at the roll call on the snowy courtyard, the shutters in Block 10 stay shut. We do not get to see the women. Again, the counting takes forever. Teas-ingly, the Krauts encircle us with their dogs. Now and again, a whip descends on a face they don't like.

After quite some time, the guards and their dogs start to walk toward the gate that separates the courtyard from the camp road. Just in front of the gate, they stop and turn around. I am watching them very carefully from the corner of my eyes. I see them chuckle. The dogs are frothing at the mouth and are pulling at their leashes.

I was expecting it. The moment they shout the order to go back to our barrack, the dogs are released. I bolt up the five steps, through the door, inside. As I run up the stairs, I hear the screams of the people who have been caught by the dogs. Unharmed and one of the first, I arrive at our bunker. A few minutes later, three bloodied victims limp inside. They are in agony. Aghast, I see that the dogs have taken large chunks out of their calves and arms. But apparently that wasn't enough. To finish the job, the Krauts have kicked them black and blue. We commiserate with the three victims. But what can we do? We have nothing to offer but a few words of consolation.

The days are passing by. Except for the recurring "festivities" at the morning roll call, during which the Germans even start to bet on which dog is going to get a prisoner first, our existence is boring and gray. After the roll call, we get a ration of bread and muddy coffee; in the evening, we get watery soup. The rest of the day we spend aimlessly at our bunker. In the meantime, I've heard whispers that the people in the basement are Polish partisans waiting for execution.

Our own future remains uncertain. We still haven't a clue what they're planning for us. Every now and again, rumors about labor camps resurface. Names, like Blech-hammer and Monowitz are mentioned. But the days are passing by, one by one, uneventfully. Fortunately, our sleeping conditions have been slightly improved. We've each gotten a horsehair blanket so that we have at least a little protection against the cold.

Then, one morning, immediately after we rise, to our amazement we are directed to the infirmary. No head count, no "festivities" today. Once inside, everybody has to roll up a sleeve and donate two pints of blood. We do not understand. Why?

It gets even crazier when, back in our block, each of us gets a quart of milk. For a while we are speculating what use our "just spilled" blood will have. An older prisoner thinks he has a plausible explanation. "The blood will be needed for the wounded Germans on the eastern front," he says. It's an absurd thought. Don't the Germans curse and revile our blood? Aren't we Jews impure, even less than pigs? Would such unworthy beings now be good enough to donate their blood to the Aryan heroes on the front line? No, it is not logical, but we cannot come up with any other explanation. At any rate, it has brought us a quiet day and a nectar-like drink.

I don't know exactly why, maybe I wasn't lining up quickly enough, or I made a sudden and thus punishable move, but at the roll call on the fifth day, I'm being kicked out of my row by the camp police. "Five lashes on the ass," one of the officers in charge shouts.

At the same moment, I am grabbed on both sides and dragged inside, through a corridor, into a space I've never seen before. With brute force, they slap me, face forward, onto an apparatus that looks like a vaulting horse. In no time, I am naked, and my feet are strapped into a wooden block attached to the floor. The guards pull both my arms forward over the "horse" as far as possible.

I know what's in store for me. A few days ago it happened to somebody else. The victim's body, pounded black and blue, had made a deep impression on us. He had received ten, twice as much as I.

The executioner gets ready to start the job. I'm shivering with fear. Just this morning I've heard that his name is Jacobi and he used to be one of the trainers of Max Schmeling, a famous boxer. He is a real animal, has a neck like an ox and hands like coal shovels.

One! With a dull thud, the pain grips my lower back. Then the sound of a long scream. It must be mine, but already numbers two, three, four, and five are administered. The pain is devastating. Then it's over. They unstrap me, drag me to the bunker, and throw me in a corner. I feel a few drops of blood dripping down my buttocks and legs and press my glowing cheeks against the cold wall. The pain of deep lashes is mixed with feelings of powerless rage and humiliation. "Beasts," I whisper, as a deep hatred begins to emerge in me. "You dirty, stinking, Krauts. . ."

Two days later, after the morning roll call, I'm ordered to fetch some blankets from Block 28. Aside from some lingering pain, I've almost completely recuperated. For the first time since our arrival, I get to see a bit more of the camp than just our block and the courtyard. I walk between Block 21 and the laundry, toward the corner of the camp where the distribution center is located.

After I report, I wait for the blankets to be fetched. Out of the blue, a prisoner approaches me. He is not very tall, but his square, muscular shape reveals the strength hidden in his body. He looks a little older than me. I immediately trust his friendly eyes and honest face.

"Dutchman?" he asks. I nod and tell him who I am. Then he introduces himself. I'm surprised to learn he is Leen Sanders from Rotterdam, the Dutch middleweight boxing champion. After I've taken delivery of my blankets, he takes me to a quiet corner so we can exchange some news. There's really not much to tell, since I've spent the past year and a half in Westerbork as a prisoner. On my part, I ask Leen if he knows what's going to happen to us. He tells me that without any doubt we will be put to hard labor in one of the projects outside the camp. But he explains that newcomers usually have to stay in quarantine for a few days to prevent the danger of infection.

I'm not sure what to think of his answer, but somehow he sounds reassuring. "Are there any more Dutch in your block?" he asks. When I tell him there are a few more of us in the bunker, he tells me to wait a second. He disappears in a flash and returns almost immediately. From under his coat and pants, he takes some food, after he's made sure no one can see us.

I can hardly believe my eyes. There are even some apples. "How the . . . ?" But I don't get the chance to finish my question. "Don't ask," Leen says. "Just promise me to share it with your friends." Apparently I keep staring at him all that time because, as he points at the delicacies, he says, "Just a matter of organization, boy, just a matter of organization .. ."

I thank Leen from the bottom of my heart and hide everything in my clothes. With a warm and friendly handshake, he says good-bye and disappears on the camp road.

Back in Block 11, I quickly deliver the blankets and hurry upstairs. Without the others noticing, I tell Eddie and Walter what has just happened to me. They are delighted over all these goodies. In the evening, under cover of darkness, we relish our festive meal in a corner of our bunker. I still have Leen Sanders's image in my head as I snuggle up under my blanket. What a great person! For the first time since I've arrived in this godforsaken place, I've encountered some human kindness.

❖ THE WHEELBARROW ❖

On the morning of the ninth or tenth day of our stay in Block 11, the moment finally arrives. Winter is retreating. The temperature is above freezing. Rainstorms, hail, and wet snow alternate and turn everything into a muddy mess. Standing in the courtyard for the early-morning count and quickly getting soaked and cold, twenty prisoners are taken aside. I'm one of them. As the others are driven back to Block 11, we start to march from the courtyard toward the camp road. A tarpaulin-covered truck, engine running, is waiting for us.

Two heavily armed SS officers who are forming some sort of gate at the back of the truck curse and chase us into the truck. Walter Sanders and I are the only ones left of our close-knit Bauer group. We huddle together, afraid of what may happen next. The truck starts to move at high speed, and soon we pass through the gate of the camp. We drive over bumpy, winding roads, tossed about like dice.

After about twenty minutes, the truck suddenly comes to a standstill. We jump off and line up, then look around and see that we are in a camp with dozens of big wooden barracks. Not too far from us a number of prisoners are struggling to push loaded wheelbarrows. The wheels are much too small and sink into the wet cinders on the ground. We immediately sense that this is a deliberate and premeditated attempt to torture and break both the prisoners' strength and any hint of resistance. They're trudging slowly past us, paying no attention to the newcomers. In dull resignation, their emaciated bodies stagger under their much too heavy load.

Suddenly, one of them collapses and drops in the mud with his wheelbarrow. It's amazing what kicking boots can do: He gets back on his feet. But after ten more yards he falls again and remains motionless. Beating and kicking no longer have any effect. At the order of a guard, some prisoners take him by his arms and legs and drop him by the roadside near a barrack. Nobody even looks at the victim; the work just goes on.

Moments later we are marched past the fallen prisoner, a motionless little heap of striped camp attire with bony limbs sticking out. His head is tilted backward and has a yellowish color. His cap has slid off. If the man is not already dead, he will be soon for sure. A bit farther down, as still as the man, is his wheelbarrow, stuck in the mud.

By way of introduction to our new housing, we are of course counted. After quite a while, they tell us we are now in labor camp Monowitz, a special unit outside Auschwitz. We will be assigned to one of the many labor units the next day.

Following the roll call, I report to my assigned barrack. It's a big shed with dozens of bunk beds. The elder shows me my top bunk and tells me how to make my bed in the morning. It has to be done in military fashion so that the pillow, the blanket, and the straw sack are exactly in line with the other beds. Every morning they measure it with some kind of yardstick. If somebody's bed is not exactly the way it is supposed to be, he can expect a fair drubbing. "Understood?" I nod.

Toward the evening the labor units return one by one to the camp. I can hardly believe my eyes. In no time, the place is teeming with people.

Sometime thereafter, slightly unsure what to do, I go to the "soup" line with my plate. When I try to join the end of the line, the other waiting prisoners push and shove me to the front. I soon notice why. The back of the line gets to eat the bottom of the pot where the soup is thicker and more nutritious.

As I eat my watery soup, I tell myself not to be intimidated tomorrow. I am young and strong. I am sure that I can conquer a spot at the end of the line.

When I return to my bunk that night, I meet my neighbor. He is a handsome Polish Jew named Aron. He is rather small, with dark, curly hair and behavior that is a bit effeminate. He seems to be good buddies with a big blond Polish Jew with thick, sensual lips whose name is Jankle. To each other they speak Yiddish. Initially, I can understand only the German words. But in spite of this language barrier, Aron gives me a lot of information on how the camp works. He also tells me that the name of the gigantic camp where we arrived ten days ago was Birkenau.

With increasing disbelief, I listen to his story. Thousands of people, mostly Jews, are killed there by the Germans. They are going through the chimney, Aron keeps saying over and over. At the time, I'm still not quite getting what he's trying to tell me, but I do understand that it is better to be sent to Monowitz and not to have been left behind in Birkenau.

Most prisoners here, Aron says, are working to build the Buna factory, a gigantic industrial complex about three miles from our camp. The factory is intended to provide the Germans with synthetic rubber. Furthermore, thousands of prisoners of war and civilian laborers from the area are working at Buna. Every morning before five, long lines leave Monowitz for Buna, where they arrive around six. They return at around six in the evening.

Aron gives me a good suggestion. When I go to sleep, wrap my spoon, plate, feet covers, and leftover bread under my pillow so that no one can touch them. We keep whispering for a long time in the dark. Indefatigably and patiently he answers my many questions about my new "home." When we finally lie down, I can hardly fall asleep. The images and impressions of this first day in Monowitz dance in my head. I keep seeing the wheelbarrow on its side in the mud.

A loud bell wakes me up. The lights are switched on, and everybody has started like maniacs to shake blankets, make beds, and get dressed. Instinctively, I jump up and copy everything the other prisoners are doing. A suffocating cloud of dust pervades the barracks as we rush outside in the direction of the toilets and washbasins. Quickly washing my face and upper body with ice-cold water, I keep my clothes and other possessions tightly between my knees.

Only a few minutes after waking up, I'm standing in line to get bread and coffee. Not too far away, I see Aron and Jankle. When Aron sees me, he gives me a thumbs-up, signifying I've done well so far.

During the roll call, I see the entire population of Monowitz for the first time. Row after row of colorless human beings stand silently in the dim morning air. The steam from our bodies that rises up in the damp, cold April morning starts to form a gray cloud in the black sky above our heads and gives the place an almost surrealistic look. I'm assigned to one of the construction units for Buna, and we start our march to the factory.

The moment we approach the camp gate, sounds of music greet us. To my amazement, left of the gate I see an orchestra comprised of prisoners playing march music as the units leave. The happy tunes sounding in the early morning evoke an incredible feeling of sadness in me. In these desolate surroundings of barbed wire and watchtowers, the music is like an echo of an unreachable and almost forgotten world.

"Arbeit macht frei," labor liberates, reads the curse above our heads as we march through the gate. The first morning light has colored the gigantic factory buildings and chimneys, covering the entire skyline when we arrive at Buna.

A bit later, I'm digging trenches for the foundation of a new factory building. We have only just begun when we are ordered to return our shovels and go to another place down the road. There, on one of the side branches of the railroad, are a number of Russian railroad cars filled with bags of cement that have to be unloaded by us. Some people are lucky enough to get into the cars and push the bags forward. I'm out of luck. Along with others, I have to take them on my shoulders. Under these bags weighing more than a hundred pounds we stagger to the building site, drop the bags, and hurry back for the next load.

We don't get a moment's rest. Under pressure of the SS, who are flogging to their hearts' content, the kapo keeps pushing us harder and harder. The speed and weight of the load are getting murderous. After an hour, I'm completely exhausted, and a thick crust of cement dust and sweat has formed on my neck, irritating it until it bleeds. When it starts to drizzle in the afternoon, it is as if I'm wearing a concrete collar. The pain is almost unbearable. But no matter how bad and exhausted I feel, I know I have to go on because the whips and the boots are relentlessly doing their work. Around me, one after the other collapses. Mercilessly, they are brought back on their feet.

"Faster! Faster!" It sounds all the time. Then one of us remains still. A guard, whose name I later find out is Muhlstein, rushes over and starts to pound the man with his stick. "Get up, you filthy Jew." Like an animal gone berserk, he keeps pounding the body on the ground. But it's in vain; death has already taken our comrade out of his suffering.

In the evening, as we stagger back to Monowitz, we drag three dead and four very ill people along with us. They're suspended between us, arms pulled over our shoulders, feet dragging the ground. A broken man, I line up for the soup, no longer strong enough even to fight for a spot in the back of the line. I'm hardly able to take in my watery ration as I seat myself in a quiet corner in the barrack.

Later, on my bed in the dark, I whisper to Aron, "If I have to unload cement bags again tomorrow, I won't survive." He puts a comforting hand on my shoulder. "Try to get into a better unit as soon as possible," he says. "You have to establish links with prominent people, those who are better off in the camp. They are influential."

A sigh of relief, as the next morning at Buna we're directed to dig trenches. No cement bags. Even though my body still aches from yesterday's labor, I start to dig diligently. It is hard, but easier than carrying the cement. But still, people are dying. Prisoners who are already weakened cannot survive this physical exertion and are battling death from start to finish. Our tormentors know this all too well, and with a satanic pleasure they keep hitting and kicking the weak ones until they just drop dead.

I'm working as hard as I can in order to avoid this torture. At one point, when I look up, I see an older prisoner of our unit standing in front of me. He's leaning on the shaft of his shovel and shaking his head. "You've got to work with your eyes, my boy, with the eyes," he says. When I give him a puzzled look, he explains, "It's better to work only when the guards are around." I follow the advice of this old pro and soon notice that by pausing regularly I don't have to exhaust myself, so I can preserve my strength.

That evening, after the meal-I did manage to get some thick soup—I get acquainted with a young Pole from Krakow. He tells me he regularly receives packages of food from his family. Therefore, he is privileged because not only does he eat better but he also trades the good stuff on the black market in the camp. He tells me that he's looking for someone to wash his clothes on Sunday, in exchange for his ration of bread. I don't hesitate a second and immediately offer my service. Within an hour, two more Poles request me to do their laundry in exchange for bread.

I excitedly tell Aron that night that, on my third day in Monowitz, I have managed to find a little job. My life, so hopeless only yesterday, seems to have regained some perspective-at least for the time being.

❖ THE SICK BAY ❖

I've been working at the trenches for several days when I learn that my friend Walter Sanders has got himself an interesting little job at Buna. Walter lives in a different barrack, and I haven't seen him or talked with him in a few days. At the midday break, which always lasts exactly thirty minutes, I see him walking right past the spot where we work. As we start talking, he tells me he has ended up as a blacksmith at a field shop close by. His work consists mainly of forging angle irons for the T beams for the high-rise construction.

"If you want to come by during lunch break for something warm to eat, don't hesitate," he says, beaming from ear to ear. "A warm meal?" I ask amazed. "Sure," he says, "but bring something to roast." The next day we are surreptitiously barbecuing some turnips on the grill that sits over the fire of his workshop. It's delicious. I intend to spend my lunch break there as often as possible.

One day as I get up I notice that my right lower leg is painfully swollen. I can hardly stand or walk on it. Still, I go to Buna and work on the trenches as best I can. But the pain increases and the swelling gets worse. During a quiet moment, when our guards are not around, I show my swollen leg to Herbert Bucholz, a young man from Frankfurt whom I work with. The sight of my leg noticeably frightens him, and he tells me to see the doctor as soon as I get back to Monowitz. "It's phlegmon," he says, "a dangerous infection. Do not ignore it."

That evening I report to the camp hospital. It is teeming. Prisoners with a variety of complaints waiting in long lines outside the barrack for their turn to be examined by one of the doctors. A lot of them are in bad shape and are sitting on the ground shivering with fever. They have almost transparent, yellowish faces, and they are so emaciated their skin stretches tautly over their bones. These apathetic, moving human skeletons, with one foot already in the grave, show not the slightest interest in their surroundings.

Finally, it's my turn. The doctor, a Jewish prisoner himself, quickly looks at my leg. "Fever?" he asks. "No, no fever." From a brown jar, he smears some ointment on the dark brown swollen infection and then puts a paper bandage on it. "Come back tomorrow," he says. The next day my lower leg is almost as big as my thigh, and the pain is excruciating. I have barely been able to sustain the hard labor at the construction site. Hours of working at the trenches are pure torture. Literally on my last leg, I drag myself back to Monowitz. Sick and shivering, I go to the same doctor. "I have a fever," I tell him before he even asks anything. When he takes off the bandage, I see a jellylike mess, a cake of pus and blood. "To the hospital," he says, after cleaning the wound and replacing the bandage.

In the huge sick bay, with hundreds of patients, a nurse assigns me a bed. Unlike in my own barrack, I have to share my bed with another prisoner. As I look around the badly lit space, I get scared. I'm surrounded by emaciated skeletons. The sounds of the moaning, delirious sick, and the rattling of dying people, are everywhere. The stench of festering wounds and the smell of bodies infected by sickness make for an unbearable atmosphere.

The man who's sharing my bed is surrounded by a deathly odor, and I'm trying desperately to stay away from him. I feel I'm in the portico of death and realize that I have to get away from here as soon as I can, no matter what.

As the night sets in and all but a few lights have been turned off, I listen to the sounds around me, wide awake and at the edge of my bed. In the middle of the night-I haven't slept a wink-a ghostlike figure appears in the room. It's a nurse, wheeling a cart between the beds. Now and then, he stops and shakes a motionless body. When there's no sign of life, he moves the cart closer and rolls the body onto it. Everything goes on very quietly and obviously routinely. As soon as the cart is full, the nurse leaves. Soon he returns with an empty cart and resumes where he left off.

A few more times in the late night he passes by with his macabre load. Then it's light. As soon as I get the chance, I let the nurse know that I feel a lot better and I am ready to leave the infirmary. I'm telling the truth. Indeed, a small miracle has happened. My fever is gone, and the applied ointment has stopped the oozing from the ulcer on my leg. The swelling has gone down remarkably. The nurse doesn't seem to have any problem with me leaving and even puts a new bandage on my leg.

Completely elated, I go outside. The rest of the day is free, and I can walk around the camp. I'm lucky, because tomorrow is Sunday, so I can give my leg an extra day's rest.

As I'm cautiously walking through the camp that afternoon, I hear violin music, and a dark gypsy appears. I've heard about him, but to see this troubadour live is quite an experience. Jakub is his name, a gifted musician who plays in the band at the camp gate every morning. He has permission to wander freely around the camp and to play his sometimes sad, sometimes gay music. He stops briefly in front of me and plays me what looks like a personal serenade. His pitch-black eyes reflect his fiery temper. Now and then he keeps them closed for seconds, as if his music were taking him to faraway places that only he can recollect.

A bit later I see him go into the sick bay. Yes, if there's one place where people have a need for the consolation of some music, that surely is it.

I enter the barrack where the camp store is. I have not been there before, but I've heard you can buy clay soap and Magorka, a low-quality tobacco made of the stems of the tobacco plant. Prisoners who work at Buna, Aron told me yesterday, get a voucher at the end of each work week; it's the equivalent of currency in the camp. The voucher for the Jews is printed on a little yellow piece of cardboard and represents a value of two and a half marks.

After the evening's usual soup, I go to the sick bay to get a fresh bandage. The wound has started to ooze again, but my leg looks a lot better than yesterday. I'm going to have to get the bandage changed a few more times over the next couple of days. I am well on my way to recovery.

In the middle of the night, I wake up. Aron has come into my bed and snuggled up. He's panting softly. Surprised, I notice how his hand glides down my belly and grabs my penis. I shiver and am ashamed to see that I'm getting an erection almost immediately. For some reason, I don't object to this unexpected intimacy and allow Aron to masturbate me with his expert hands. But before bringing me to a climax, he suddenly lets go and starts to masturbate himself. The moment he starts to groan, I turn away from him, to let him know that despite the fact I did get aroused by his touch, I'm not really interested in homosexual encounters. Without speaking a word, we lie there in our separate beds, each ashamed in his own way.

Tomorrow is Sunday, a day of rest even in Monowitz.

❖ SELECTION ❖

On my first Sunday in Monowitz, after the morning roll call, I go to do the laundry for the Poles. The place is extremely drafty, there is mud everywhere, and it smells like a sewer. There are placards with educational texts on the walls. In the context of our miserable circumstances, they look hypocritical and ludicrous at the same time. One of them reads: "One louse, your Death!"

With my little piece of gray soap purchased at the camp store, I try to scrub the clothes clean as best as possible. The soap has absolutely no lather, and like crazy I rub one piece of clothing against another attempting to remove stains and mud. In the afternoon I deliver the clean clothes to my clients, who, after a thorough inspection, are very satisfied with my work. Overly glad, I take my extra portions of bread and hide them safely under my clothes.

In the soup line, they are talking about a soccer game. A soccer game, here, in Monowitz? I can hardly believe it. Yes, just like in Westerbork, they play real soccer matches on Sundays. On the cinders of the courtyard, they set up real goalposts with nets. The players are dressed in proper soccer attire, and the game is supervised by a referee and two linesmen. One of the nearby barracks is used as a locker room for the players and the officials, and there are showers after the game.

They tell me there is a Jewish team, Yellow Triangles; a political prisoners' team, Red Triangles, and a criminals' team, Green Triangles. To my surprise, I hear that Bobby Prijs from ZFC, the Dutch League team, is playing for the Jewish team as their right winger. I have to get onto that team, I think to myself. Don't I have a reasonable record in soccer? Two years ago I was playing in my club's first team and was even selected for the Dutch youth team. I mention it to Herbert Bucholz. When he hears all this and learns of my strong desire to play on the Jewish team, he's pleasantly surprised. "That would be nice," he says. "Maybe we'll get to play each other. I'm playing for the Red Triangles. I'll talk about it with the camp elder. He is the man in charge."

That afternoon, as I'm watching from the real chalk sidelines, I notice there is a lot of interest in the match. Hundreds of prisoners have come to watch the sports event. Even the SS is there. Smiling and aware of their own importance, they are seated on specially built bleachers. The rest of the spectators are making sure to stay as far away from this "grandstand" as possible. Only the camp elder is showing off in the immediate vicinity of the SS. He obviously wants to be seen. He walks about in his tailor-made dark blue coat and hat, like the mayor of Monowitz. Shiny boots underscore his desire to be important and identify him with his SS masters. Through years of stays in a variety of labor and concentration camps, he has worked himself to the top of the camp hierarchy.

I ask another prisoner next to me if the Jehovah's Witnesses, who are adorned with purple triangles, and the homosexuals with their pink triangles, have their own teams. "No," he replies, "the Jehovahs don't participate in these profane events, and the 'pinkies' are not allowed for obvious reasons." I don't understand. "Well, they like to attack from behind," he grins. "They are called the one seventy-fives, which refers to an article in the penal code that makes homosexuality an unlawful act." I also learn that the Green Triangles are the seniors in the camp; you can tell by their low registration number. Generally, they are a little older than us, and their soccer results reflect this. They tend to lose big.

I follow the match with close attention. Indeed, the level of the game is quite high, even though the speed is low because of the bad physical condition of the players. During the break, I gather my courage and walk to the camp elder. He gives me with an icy, arrogant look when I tell him I have played in the highest league and the national youth team of Holland. "Could I possibly play on the Jewish team?" I ask him in my most friendly German. "Not a chance," he bites back, "and get the hell away from me or I'll kick your ass!" "Too bad," I say politely and smile. Wisely, I retreat and start watching the second half.

Maybe I shouldn't have approached the man, I tell myself, maybe I've really wasted my chances. Fortunately, there is still Herbert, who promised to recommend me. All my hope lies with him now. I don't know how he did it, but a few days later, as we march our unit to Buna, Herbert tells me I've been admitted to the Jewish team. I'm overjoyed. It means I can show my soccer talent in the upcoming match. It's even better because I will be playing against Herbert: the Jews versus the political prisoners. I'm really looking forward to it and can hardly wait for Sunday.

I'm no longer worried about my leg. The recovery has been fast, and I'm no longer in pain. The only fear I have is new injuries or sicknesses that could prevent my first appearance in the team.

We get back exhausted to Monowitz that night. After we have dropped the weight of the dead from our shoulders, there's a surprise for us. After our soup, we are ordered to go to our barracks. Immediately a nervous anticipation spreads through the camp, and in our barrack the atmosphere is one of light panic.

Everywhere, small groups of prisoners are gesticulating and talking to one another. I ask Hugo, a Czech, thin as a rail, what's going on. "Selection," he says with a fearful look. Searching for words, in bits and pieces he explains in his broken German that the SS will soon be inspecting us. I can tell from the story that, under the guise of a check on pubic lice, the overall fitness of the prisoners will be judged. Those who are designated "incapable to work" will be registered by their number. The next day, they will be deported to Birkenau.

"What happens then?" I want to know. Hugo raises both hands. "Through the chimney, everybody dead, everybody dead," he cries desperately. I look at him in disbelief. Through the chimney?

Suddenly, the uneasiness that pervades the barrack gets a grip on me, too. I realize I've heard the name Birkenau more and more over the last few days. The wind has been from the west, and now and then a penetrating stench hangs all over Monowitz. The prisoners who have been here a bit longer are making eerie remarks. "We'll all go through the chimney sooner or later!"

I've always shrugged my shoulders about these words and refused to take them literally. But at this moment, seeing how everyone reacts to the upcoming selection, I too get this feeling of approaching doom.

Hugo grabs my arm, and his eyes almost pierce through me. "Honestly, how do I look? Am I too thin? What do you think?" From a bony face, I see two desperate eyes staring at me. I smile quickly and offer some encouraging words. "Oh, you look fine. Ask the others, they'll agree." He nods briefly, as if to confirm my words, and heads to a group nearby to ask the same questions.

I look at my own body. Is it my imagination or have I all of a sudden lost a bit of weight? It seems I was a lot heavier yesterday. Could that have changed so rapidly? I'm not quite sure, so I look for Aron and tell him I'm worried. "Don't be a fool," he says. "If you don't make the selection, they can ship the entire camp to Birkenau." Aron's firm words are making me feel a lot easier, but a sense of insecurity and fear remain.

The waiting seems to take forever, and the tension in the barrack grows by the minute. Two SS officers, accompanied by the barrack elder, enter and take a seat behind a desk. At some distance, we are waiting, completely nude, for things to happen. I feel goose bumps over my entire body, and I tremble nervously.

Some commands are shouted, and prisoners start to go past the desk. Some are pretending, as best they can, to look strong and healthy;

they're walking with straight backs steadfastly past the probing eyes. But the inspectors cannot be fooled: They can see at a glance who'll pass their test and who won't. The odd prisoner is ordered to stand still for further inspection. A moment of lethal tension follows, when he continues. We stretch our necks to see if his number is jotted down.

Then, suddenly, it's my turn. A gesture to come forward. As I approach, it feels like stepping into another world. Distance and time evaporate into these all-encompassing seconds. Slowly, as in a feverish dream, the walls are flowing by me. When I finally touch the walls on the opposite side of the barrack, I return to reality. It's over. I take a deep breath. All fear and tension dissipate. I'm convinced all went well for me. I quickly get dressed and rejoin the group.

When the selection is over and the SS has gone to the next barrack, chaos erupts. Everybody wants to know from everybody else whether his number has been written down. "Did they take my number? No? Are you sure?" Even though we've clearly seen some numbers being jotted down, we lie through our teeth. Everybody gets the same answer: No, they didn't write your number down. Hugo, like myself, has gotten through. He had to stop at the desk, they had some questions, but I did not see them write anything.

Like many of us, I barely sleep that night. Wide awake on my straw bed, I stare in the dark. I can hear that Aron is also awake. "What exactly will happen tomorrow?" I whisper. Aron explains that the barrack elder will have the list and announce who will not be required to join his work unit that day. Like always, he will then try to soothe the victims, saying they'll probably be put to work somewhere else.

But everybody who has been here awhile knows they will be taken to Birkenau that same morning. Only their clothes will be shipped back to Monowitz that night.

❖ Benno ❖

It is a strange sensation when I march to Buna on Monday morning in a new unit. I'm really happy to have been assigned to Unit 186; we're one of the sweep teams. We're only thirty prisoners and are headed by a kapo called Alexander, whom everybody calls Xandl. He is a tiny little man from Vienna. It's hard to imagine that he is capable of brute force.

On our way, I get to know a certain Benno Klein, the writer of our unit. He is taller and quite a bit older than me. He must be about forty. He looks fairly healthy and fit. As I look at him from the side, I suddenly have to think of the movie *The 39 Steps* by Alfred Hitchcock, which I saw in Nij-megen shortly before the war. In that movie, a man on the train is missing the top of his left index finger, exactly like Benno. But that's about the only similarity. Contrary to the creep in the movie, Benno appears to be a great companion.

I immediately like him and ask him about his job as a "writer." He tells me in juicy Flemish that he really has a cushy job. At the end of every day, he has to make a report concerning the work our unit has done that day. That's all that is required. The rest of the day he can do as he pleases, if he's smart. Benno grew up in Poland but came to Antwerp long before the war.

Casually, he tells me he speaks seven languages: Yiddish, Polish, Dutch, German, Russian, French, and English. Since he has quite a few "commercial" contacts with civilian laborers at Buna, this comes in very handy. He hints that he can thus "organize" a lot of things. Benno tells me what this sweep job is all about. I will be working at a carbide factory where we will be sweeping several floors. This is music to my ears.

"But you have to be careful, little man, because one nail under your shoe and you'll have an explosion," he warns. He tells me that just recently, a few prisoners were killed by such an explosion. "You won't have any problem with Xandl. As soon as he gets there, he disappears and reappears only in the evening," he says. The silhouettes of the factory buildings are showing on the horizon. Another fifteen minutes and we'll be there.

"How did you get into this unit?" he asks me. "Via soccer," I say with a smile. I tell him enthusiastically about my debut with the Jewish team the previous day.

Filled with pride, I had entered the field with my teammates. It had been a great feeling to substitute the squeaky-clean, colorful soccer attire and real leather shoes for the smelly prison clothes adorned with the hated number. For the first time in a long while I had not felt like a number, an animal in the herd. With complete dedication I threw myself into the match, and it felt like time had been turned back a few years. Briefly, I had forgotten everything around me. It had been a fantastic match.

We had been behind but came back every time. Bobby Prijs, our left wing, had been playing like a real star. He had tied the score with a hard, diagonal shot. 1-1. In the second half, we once again fell behind, but Bobby gave me a golden opportunity, and I scored the tying point. Then, during the last minutes, I scored the winner with a long-distance shot. As we walked off the field and the applause engulfed us, I knew I was famous. I could not have wished for a better debut. Everybody congratulated me after the game.

Herbert Bucholz, whom we had given a hard time as the left defender for the Red Triangles, came over to me immediately after we had showered. "You were great," he said. "I'll have a chat tonight to see

By Louis de Wijze

if we can get you in a better unit." And so he had done. Before we went to bed, he came over to tell me to report to Unit 186 the next morning. "And that I did," I smiled to Benno. With a big smile, he listened to the entire story. "Welcome to the club," he says as we enter Buna.

I barely arrive on the first floor of the factory with my broom when the others tell me it's very dangerous and explosive around here. I get some advice and instructions and go to work.

The first floor of the factory has the ovens in which calcium and coal are heated to form carbide. From the inside, the ovens are isolated by a special sort of brick. The space is connected to an enormous factory hall in which several labor units are put to work. I soon notice that this sweep job, compared to my previous job in the trenches, is a breeze. Of course, the same rule applies here-"work with your eyes"-but other than that, the atmosphere is almost relaxed. People talk more than they work. An added advantage is that Aron and Jankle are also employed in this unit. It makes it a bit easier to get used to this new environment.

That morning, the foreman of the factory, a man called Vraneck, comes to inspect our work. He is a German from Breslau, quite ordinary looking but with a calculating and cruel look about him. I don't like him. When he hears I'm Dutch, he suddenly becomes interested.

Quasi-amicably he tells me that two years ago he worked in The Hague. Except for some cursing and foul language, he doesn't seem to have picked up much Dutch. He seems to be very proud of this. He pronounces the word *Gadver-damme* (Goddamn it) and revels in the way he is able to say the very guttural Dutch G. That day I have a few more encounters with him, and every time he sees me, he shouts "You, Dutchman, Gggodverdamme," and then bursts out laughing. Even though I don't feel at ease with his coarse approach, I don't show him any of that. I keep smiling and pretend to like his "humor." I wonder what Vraneck did in The Hague. It wouldn't surprise me if he had worked for the security police. When I mention it to Aron and Jankle, they tell me he is not that bad; they've never seen him hit or kick anybody. "Just don't get in his way, and he won't be any trouble," they reassure me.

Work is light, and the hours pass by quickly to the lunch break. At twelve, as we walk to the shed where bread and coffee are distributed, we encounter scores of prisoners of war, forced and civilian laborers. Just like us, they're allowed a half-hour lunch break. Benno had told me in the morning that there were about thirty thousand people working here. Thirty thousand! That is the complete population of a small town! As I sit down in a corner to eat my bread, I have an opportunity to observe my surroundings.

The factory grounds are now teeming with people. It looks like an anthill. Even the organization at Buna resembles that of an industrious ant colony. Everything is structured down to the most minute detail. There are guards, and there is a strict discipline to control the masses. However, there is one big difference: Ants are instinctively forced to work and sacrifice themselves for the greater good, up to the point of mass suicide. We, on the contrary, who are endowed with our own free will and feelings, are working because we have been enslaved by an aggressive minority.

The afternoon is as easy as the morning. I use the time to find out as much as I can about my new work situation. I find out that Vraneck's boss is a certain Dr. Hinder, a technical engineer by profession, an overweight man in his forties who has his office here in Buna and coordinates the entire construction. "He is one of the worst anti-Semites. Stay away from him," Jankle warns on our walk back to Monowitz that evening. This time, there are no sick or dead to carry with us.

❖ THE FIRST ❖ AIR STRIKES

One day I start a conversation with two English prisoners of war who work at Buna, Robert Wiggins and Jimmy Robertson. Both are very sympathetic, and the three of us like to talk and exchange the latest news. I hear that the POWs are being kept in a stalag approximately a third of a mile from Buna. In flagrant violation of the Geneva Convention, which forbids forced labor by POWs, thousands of captured allied soldiers have been put to work at Buna.

Except for strict internment rules, Robert and Jimmy are reasonably okay in their stalag. Every now and then, through mediation of the Red Cross, they get food packages, which enable them to improve their diet considerably. With these they also get cigarettes and thus do not have to smoke Magorka tobacco rolled in newspaper. When I hear this, I get a brilliant idea. Could they save their cigarette butts and bring them to Buna for me? I explain that I will take the leftover tobacco and sell this on the black market in Monowitz in order to get bread or soup.

They both promise to collect and bring me the cigarette butts. They're obviously pleased to be able to do something for me. When we say good-bye, Robert quickly shakes my hand and gives me a little something wrapped in paper. It turns out to be a piece of chocolate. Salivating, I slowly let it melt in my mouth. Hours later, I can still taste the heavenly flavor on my tongue.

The English keep their word. They keep bringing me, almost daily, the desired merchandise, and regularly in the evenings I can be found at the camp corner where the black market transactions take place.

My merchandise is in great demand, because the quality difference between the English tobacco and the Magorka is enormous. I quickly learn to be firm in my negotiations and not to be tempted to accept a low bid. It often happens that my asking price is deemed much too high, but I don't react when the bidder walks away. I know he'll be back with a new bid, and eventually I'll get my price.

The tobacco business that I have started, thanks to my English friends, enables me to double my daily rations and thus considerably enhances my chances for survival. Without the extra portions in addition to the daily minimum, the outlook would have been very bleak for me. That little bit of bread, the sliver of margarine, and the muddy soup with a tiny piece of meat or potato, if you're lucky, is absolutely insufficient to preserve one's strength and survive. Every day, scores of prisoners succumb to malnutrition, exhaustion, and physical violence. We see their bodies dragged through the camp roads; they are barely able to stand up for the roll call. At night in the barrack, I can hear them hallucinate and groan. In the morning, trucks loaded with corpses drive to the crematoria of Birkenau.

Many of our comrades disappear without us noticing immediately. You suddenly realize they are no longer there at the roll call and not in the barrack. Nobody can tell you whether they died at night or were taken to the sick bay.

Some mornings we see them hanging like scarecrows on the electric fence that surrounds our camp. They made the choice to walk deliberately into the deadly wires rather than suffer anymore at the hands of their tormentors. It is an horrific sight: their bodies singed and stiff. The Germans deliberately leave the bodies hanging for a while just to show how effective the camp security is.

My work at Unit 186 is a relatively bright spot in this hellhole. Not only is the work light, but as time passes, the supervision is becoming flexible enough to allow us a certain amount of freedom.

Sometimes, when the kapo sends me to pick up some materials or tools, I wander about the factory for a long time unnoticed. On one of those "trips," I talk to a civilian worker and find out he works with a Dutchman from Nijmegen. He asks me to follow him to one of the factory buildings. Then I have to wait a minute. Soon he returns with somebody I immediately recognize. It is the son of a pastry maker I know from Nijmegen. Briefly I feel the joy of recognition, and he has the same enthusiastic reaction. But immediately thereafter we feel embarrassed because he works as a volunteer for the Germans, and he can see that I'm a camp prisoner. Soon our conversation grinds to a halt. We exchange a few more generalities and then quickly say goodbye. "See you in Nijmegen," I call as we return to our respective work sites. "Who knows," he responds in a voice that doesn't exude a lot of confidence.

A few days later, as I am in a building that's slightly away from our work site, having a chat with a Greek fellow, all of a sudden all hell breaks loose. Mortified, we seem to be glued to the spot. The ground beneath our feet undulates. It feels like an earthquake. At the same time, our eardrums are pounded by a series of explosions.

Before I know it, I'm being lifted off the ground in a cloud of dust and debris. In a flash, I see one of the factory walls blown away like a piece of paper. "What happened?" I ask two men who are leaning over me. I don't know where I am or why I am on the floor. A heavy load sits on my chest. The men are starting to pull the weight off of me. "What happened?" I ask, this time in German. Buna has been bombed, somebody replies.

Carefully, some helping hands are pulling me in a sitting position. I see the lifeless body of the Greek lying next to me. "He was lying on top of you," the same voice continues. "That saved you." I'm starting to feel nauseated, my head is spinning, and I'm hurting everywhere. "Can you walk? Did you break any bones?" they ask. I get up cautiously and try to walk a few steps. Everything seems to function normally, but for a few bruises and scratches. Again, I look at the Greek. It could have been the other way around, I now realize. He is lying still on his back, eyes half closed. It's like he's about to ask what's happened, just as I did.

As the search for survivors and victims continues in full force, I start to make my way back over the scattered debris to the intact carbide factory. After a few hours of taking stock of the damage, it turns out that dozens of people have been killed. The sections of the complex that were about to go into production seem to have been the main targets of the Allied forces. As if they knew exactly ...

For the first time in weeks, our units had to drag back a number of dead to Monowitz. Limping, but on my own, I walk the three miles back to our camp. Nobody has to support me. "Don't the Americans and the English know that thousands of prisoners work at Buna?" I ask Benno, who walks next to me like always. No answer.

One morning in May, Vraneck awaits us as we arrive at the carbide factory. Instead of going to our regular spot, he directs us to a high-rise building. Apparently the rebuilding of the destroyed factory halls is not progressing fast enough, and they need extra workers to make up for lost time. Our new job consists of assembling T beams at a high elevation.

Equipped with heavy tools, we climb up the scaffolding and on instructions of the foreman take up our positions. Although the work is not heavy or difficult, most of us have great trouble with the height at which we have to work. Big cranes hoist huge iron beams through the air to us. We then have to push them into place and fix them tightly. Any hesitation or misstep can be fatal; nobody would survive a fall of fifty feet or more.

I'm not scared by nature; I did a lot of foolish things in my youth. But at this height I really have to concentrate not to make any mistakes. At times, fear really gets a grip on me. One time, just as I am trying to make a connection, I hear from way below, "You, Dutchman, why don't you jump off? It's easy. No more problems." This is followed by thunderous laughter. Apparently Vraneck had been watching me for a while and seen my moments of weakness. Fortunately, he soon leaves and I'm no longer teased. Still, it keeps bothering me, and I'm intensely happy when the day is over.

To my relief, we return to our regular job the next day. Midafternoon, Vraneck makes his appearance again. Of course, he's walking right toward me. He looks at me in thought. "You, Dutchman, have you ever worked with rabbits?" Why does he want to know? I quickly try to assess my situation. His voice had sounded normal, no cynicism or threat in there. It had seemed he had just wanted a positive answer.

I had been six years old when my parents gave me a bunny. My father himself had built a nice little hutch, complete with rack and sloping roof. The very first day, my bunny had spent more time on my lap than in his home. That night we had had brussels sprouts for dinner. I had carefully collected all the leftovers and taken them to my pet. It had been a big heap, and the animal had been munching continuously. Early the next morning I had run outside to greet my friend. All the food had been eaten. The rack was empty, and my rabbit was lying still in his straw bed, his belly all swollen. Only after my mother had made me touch the stiff cadaver did I realize my little pet was dead.

Had I ever worked with rabbits? "Yes, sir, Mr. Vraneck," I answer and tell him I have had experience with and cared for rabbits since I was a young boy.

"All right, follow me," is all he says. He takes me to a section of the Buna where I've never been before. He stops at a small stone shed. We enter what looks like a stable. Alongside the walls, three stories of big hutches have been built for a total of twelve rabbits. Halfway up there is a hayloft one can reach via a wooden ladder.

Satisfied, Vraneck looks around. Apparently everything is brand-new because it looks fresh and you can still smell the resin of the wood.

With a wide gesture, Vraneck points at the rabbits. "From today, you are responsible for my rabbits," he says, explaining what that entails.

I have to make sure the animals get their food on time and that their hutches are cleaned every day. He orders me to fatten the rabbits so they'll be nice and plump. "They're for human consumption," he says, and he looks as if he can already see the set table. I get the key to the stable, and after he has shown me where the food and tools are kept, he leaves me alone.

Minutes later I realize that I've just gotten myself a fantastic new job. Did I understand correctly? Can I, every day, do my job completely independently in this comfortable little building? Why did Vraneck choose me? Does he still have ties with Holland, his previous post? Whatever the reason, I'm not going to let go of this chance of a lifetime. I climb the ladder to the hayloft and drop in the hay.

With a deep breath I inhale the wonderful smell of the country. For minutes I just lie there, my arms stretched out wide, my eyes fixed on the beams and roof tiles.

On the way back to Monowitz, walking next to Benno, I tell him what happened to me. "You're one lucky devil," he says "but be aware Vraneck is only a messenger boy. Those rabbits belong to his boss, Dr. Hinder, I'm sure." "I could not care less," I laugh. "From now on I'm living like a king."

For a while, Benno is silent. I look at him from the side. Apparently he's thinking about my story. "I'll come and look at your little palace tomorrow morning," he says with glistening eyes. Obviously he has got an idea, but I don't ask.

Unlike other evenings on our return to the camp, we have to proceed immediately to the courtyard. Soon it is clear why.

In front of ten thousand prisoners, a gallows has been erected. Aron and Jankle had told me about the executions in Monowitz many times, but this is my first personal experience, and I'm very tense. With a lot of feel for decorum, the Krauts have summoned the camp orchestra to play some pithy marching music so as to brighten up this eerie get-together.

Suddenly, the music stops and the courtyard goes dead silent! Our stomachs all tense up. Then a loud voice over our heads announces that number such-and-such has committed a grave crime against German law and has, therefore, been condemned to hang in the name of the fuhrer.

Motionless, our bald heads down, we wait and see. In the eyes of our tormentors, we are the needed entourage to justify the unjustifiable. A short, sharp order sounds. We see two guards take a very tall prisoner, hands tied behind his back, to the scaffold. Quietly, offering no resistance, he walks along. He is almost a head taller than his guards. Again, some orders. The victim is blindfolded, and the noose goes around his neck.

As if frozen, we watch and hold our breath these last few seconds of the prisoner's life. Then, the final order. The trap door falls down and a terrible drama unfolds. Maybe the prisoner's weight compared to the height of the drop was too little, or maybe the noose was not tight enough. In any case, the hanging fails miserably.

A wave of horror goes over the courtyard as the poor fellow keeps on jerking wildly as he dangles on the rope. Like a fish on the hook, he is fighting a horrible fight with strangulation.

"The fall did not break his neck," Benno whispers to me. "Why don't they take the poor guy out of his suffering?" The Krauts are looking in amazement but are interested in the twitching victim. They could finish him off with a single shot, but it does not even seem to enter their minds. As the agony continues, the camp orchestra resumes the music and we march past the site of the execution. Even though I had intended to look straight ahead, it is as if my head is pulled away.

Slowly, the body dangles back and forth, as if blown by a light breeze. Short, shocking movements reveal the continuation of the gruesome agony. I'm looking at the purplish blue face of the dying man. His glistening eyes seem to be screaming at me. They haunt me for a long time.

❖ MY LITTLE PALACE ❖

Early the next morning, Benno visits me in my new workplace. I soon realize his interest for my "palace" is not totally unselfish. He displays a wide grin when he sees the hayloft. He tells me he's gotten acquainted with a young Polish woman who works as a civilian laborer at Buna. It would, of course, be fantastic, he says with a heavenly look, if he could "use" that hayloft every now and then. "What did you have in mind?" I ask. "Well," he laughs, "during your lunch break, when you go to pick up your bread, I will watch over your little shed." I don't mind, particularly because Benno promised me part of a lucrative business that will net me an extra ration of bread and soup.

A little after twelve, Benno and his blond Polish woman appear at the shed. Brunja is plump and very attractive. There is something sultry about her. I feel like an extra in a play when Benno formally introduces her to me. She shakes my hand with her eyes down. The softness of her hand confuses me and evokes a feeling I no longer thought I had. Briefly, but long enough to realize the sincerity, I am very jealous of Benno. How can that old man possibly have conquered such a lovely, sexy thing?

My thoughts go back to last summer in Westerbork. While my friends were playing cards, four yards away, on a lower bunk bed, I was making passionate love to a blond Russian Jewish woman on an upper bunk. She had been panting and groaning furiously. She hadn't cared at all about the card-playing spectators who had joined her every scream. Feverishly, she had brought us to a wonderful climax.

With the Polish woman so close by, I can smell the rancid scent of a bed that's been slept on and a whiff of a just-picked flower bouquet. I let go of her hand. The brief spell is broken instantly. Both my feet are back on firm Buna ground.

Both lovers are in a hurry because the lunch break is short. We agree that I'll lock the door and will be back a few minutes before the end of the break. They go inside quickly and climb the ladder to the loft. Unnoticed, I stay in the doorway for a few seconds and listen to the rustling hay and her cooing laughter. Then I step outside, quietly close the door, and turn the key.

Around four that afternoon, I go over to Benno. As the writer of our unit, he has his own office, which means a tiny wooden shed somewhere between the gigantic factory buildings. It is a very simple little office with a table, a chair, and some benches.

Before telling me about the business, Benno looks at me with piercing eyes. "Well, Louis," he says, "do you dare to take some risk, or do you shit in your pants easily?" In my youthful recklessness, I immediately assure him I'm not afraid of any danger. Benno then tells me that he has been smuggling vodka into the camp for quite a while. He's been able to get it from the civilian workers at Buna. He doesn't tell me who his contacts or the end users of the merchandise are. The only thing he wants from me is to be his courier, as of immediately.

"What does that entail?" I want to know. From the corner of the shed, he takes two bottles of vodka. He explains how to hide them, top down, in my loin area, under my clothes. That way, they'll be practically invisible in case I get checked. "The vodka supply is very large at the moment," Benno says, as if it is a done deal. "It's best to come by every afternoon around four." I hesitate. Benno is a sly one. This way, he can shift all his risk to me while cashing all the profit of the deal. On the other hand, the prospect of doubling my daily food portions is very tempting.

"Okay, I'll do it," I say. Benno hands me the two bottles, which I carefully hide under my clothes. As soon as we get back to the camp, I will give them back at a prearranged spot.

I'm quite nervous as we march back to Monowitz. All the time I have the feeling everybody can see the contraband under my clothes. And what to do if they check me at the gate? But everything goes well. Not a single complication. I deliver the bottles to the agreed spot without a problem.

I'm very happy with my work as rabbit keeper. It is an absurd situation: While most of my fellow prisoners are tortured day in and day out and return to Monowitz humiliated and exhausted, I am able to retreat to the shelter of my little palace.

A few times per week, Vraneck shows up to check my work. He inspects the cleanliness of the hutches and here and there grabs and lifts a rabbit to feel if it is oven ready. But apparently he and Dr. Hinder want well-fed animals on their plates, because without fail, he keeps thinking the rabbits are still too skinny. Maybe all the animals are destined to be the Krauts' next Christmas dinner.

At any rate, both Vraneck and I are quite pleased with my work. But he does not know that I occasionally put a male with a female. He has expressly forbidden that. Perhaps he is afraid of me starting my own illegal business. After four weeks, when the young ones are born, I put them in a far corner with their mother, where they are almost impossible to reach. Vraneck has not noticed anything so far. I am not really worried.

By Louis de Wijze

❖ INVASION ❖

It is June 6, 1944, a little after seven in the morning. I am on my way to Benno's office when this small, stocky fellow comes running at me. We've talked before, usually during lunch hour. I recognize his clothing. The forced laborers at Buna are housed with civilians in the area and wear normal blue overalls, not the striped camp gear. Many of the French are wearing their characteristic berets, and are, therefore, easily recognizable. The same goes for this little guy. But why is he so excited? He is running like a madman, gesturing with his arms, shouting from afar. I cannot understand what he is saying. But there he stands in front of me, completely out of breath.

"The invasion has started, my friend," he exclaims, as he gasps for air. Enthusiastically, he takes my arms as if to ask me to dance, here, in the middle of the camp road. Like a whirlwind he begins to tell me the Allied forces at this very moment have landed at the coast of Normandy. He heard it on the radio. Under cover of night, hundreds of converted landing boats crossed the English Channel, and tens of thousands of soldiers started their offensive against the completely surprised German defensive positions.

The Frenchman is exhilarated. He is constantly shaking my arms, just to make sure I realize how important this event is. But before I can react to this fantastic news, he runs along to bring the good news to others. Only when I see him disappear in the distance between the factory buildings do I, too, become overjoyed. Invasion in Normandy! Finally it is going to happen!

The melodious voice of the Frenchman echoes in my head like a musical refrain. My blood rushes through my veins, and I feel extremely excited. Light as a feather, I float to my friend Benno in order to have him participate in the joy of this wonderful moment. I run into his office and instantly freeze.

Benno is sitting at his table with a dark-haired young SS sergeant, both with a cup of coffee, elbows on the table. They turn their heads toward me in surprise. I just want to wheel around and run away, but Benno beckons me to come in.

I close the door behind me and approach with hesitation, constantly glancing at the German. But he seems relaxed, even friendly. My instinct tells me Benno and the man must be on good terms. Apparently slightly embarrassed with the situation, the sergeant dons his cap and says good-bye to Benno. As he exits, he nods at me in a friendly manner. Stunned and overwhelmed, I just stand there, almost brain dead.

What is going on? Am I on the right track? Have I walked into a trap with open eyes? All of a sudden there are no more differences between slaves and masters. Benno sees how puzzled I am and tells me to sit down. Once I'm seated, he explains in his own calm way that the man can be trusted completely.

The man is from Latvia and visits Benno's office regularly. They often have a glass of vodka together, talk about how homesick they are, and discuss business. "You don't have to be afraid of him, Louis. Our friend is up to his neck in the business. That alone makes him harmless." I sigh with relief.

Then I remember what brought me here in the first place and start to tell him the great news, sometimes stumbling over my own words. At the word invasion, Benno jumps out of his chair. "That's fantastic!" he yells. "Our German friends are going to have to run and hide, because the Americans are going to burn their asses, I think!"

Like two naughty schoolboys discussing the secrets of their club in their hideout, we savor this hopeful news for quite some time in the half-dark shed. Flushed with excitement, we tell each other of our plans when we get back home. In our fantasy, we paint each other a scene of scrumptious dinner tables, and beautiful full-breasted women with hot thighs.

"Come on, go back to your little palace," says Benno, who is the more sensible of the two of us. "Quite probably our guards might be a little confused this morning, which is not to our advantage. So keep your eyes and ears open." I get up and walk to the door. "Oh, by the way, I don't think I'll be visiting your palace today," he says with a smile as I leave.

As I walk to my little palace, I realize how absurd it is that we, as prisoners, in this far corner of Poland, at 7 a.m., already know the most recent and important news about the war. Most people have just woken up. In the Dutch kitchens, the old familiar sound of clanging cups and saucers has just started. Soon, at the 8 A.M. news, the Kraut-controlled news service will undoubtedly report how the German defense forces in Normandy have bravely repelled a cowardly offensive from the sea.

❖ THE OAT BIN ❖

The news of the invasion spreads through Buna and later through Monowitz like wildfire. Everyone has his own opinion. In our first euphoria, we shout to one another that it is going to be a matter of weeks, or maybe a few months maximum, and then this reign of terror may be over. But some are less optimistic. They point out how strong the German defense lines at the "Atlantic Wall" really are. The Allies may have landed, but can they break through? And what will happen to us if the Germans lose the war? Don't think Hitler will let us live. He is going to have us killed even at the last moment.

However, we are dismissing these pessimists with contempt. How can they think that way? Don't they have any hope and confidence left? But soon after June 6, the excitement of the invasion dissipates. Only sporadically do we hear about the steady, but particularly slow, advance of the Allies. The daily misery puts the occasional news from the war front on the back burner. Our fellow prisoners keep falling like flies.

The gruesome hard labor in the units continues unabated. Sickness and exhaustion are taking their toll every day. And those who do survive suffer because they continuously fear being deported to Birkenau at the next selection.

Everyone lives for himself. Our one and all-encompassing credo is: Survive! Between the outer limits of life and death; previous values and norms lose their meaning, and our spiritual baggage gradually erodes. The only norm that counts is "I." All our senses, thoughts, and deeds are used only for our own benefit. A large part of our previous vocabulary has disappeared. New meanings are filling the empty spaces. Nobody ever again talks about "stealing." The way we manage to obtain extra bread, feet covers, better wooden shoes, or objects to swap through all kinds of creative ways is now called "organizing," irrespective of whether you can call it "legal."

That is how we live from day to day, from one piece of bread to the next bit of soup. We don't think any farther than tomorrow; yesterday is gone. And when Sunday comes and your unit, thank God, doesn't have to work that day, the hours slip away like water in your hand. Those who still can, walk in small groups through the camp. One day without yelling kapos, beating guards. But for most people, a single day to regain one's strength is insufficient. Sunday, for a lot of people, is just a day to start worrying about Monday.

When I put on my squeaky clean, freshly ironed soccer attire and walk on the pitch with my teammates, I feel incredibly privileged compared with the masses. During that hour and a half of sports competition, nothing matters but the leather ball and the goal, just like old times.

I was only seventeen. It was 1939, and part of the first core team of Quick Nijmegen had been mobilized. Young, talented players had therefore got their chance earlier than anticipated to play in the first team. I had been one of them. The newspaper had called me a Sunday's child. The very first ball I had received, a free kick twenty yards from the goalposts, had immediately resulted in a goal.

Two years later, after the Germans had occupied Holland and had started to tighten the noose on the Jews, I had played my last match. With a select team from Nijmegen, we had battled a similar team from Arnhem. The entire German occupation elite had been watching from the grandstand. Arnhem's city commander had been there, too. I had been running my socks off and had worked extremely hard. I chuckled at the thought that the Krauts had been applauding a Jewish boy.

Soccer was everything for me; it ruled my life. I had been over-joyed to be able to continue playing my favorite sport in transit camp Westerbork. It had given me courage and strength, self-confidence and self-respect. And even now, six hundred miles from home, with death all around me, I can still totally immerse myself in the game.

For an hour and a half there are no orders, no sticks, no gallows. Immensely enjoying the thunderous applause, and almost afloat on the cheers, I just let myself go. After every match won, I am thor-oughly convinced this hell we live in soon will be behind me like a bad dream.

Not far from the barrack where the central kitchen is located there is a bordello that they call the Puf. I can't believe my ears when somebody tells me that twenty-five women are housed in a some-what smaller barrack. They offer their services to the prisoners for money. We Jews are not permitted there. Only political prisoners and criminals have admission to the Puf-if they feel like it and have the strength.

I've heard that special vouchers for three or four marks are avail-able. There is not much more to learn about it, and frankly, I'm not that interested. Except for a small group of prominent people, hardly anybody has any erotic feelings left in him. Camp life has made the inhabitants so numb that the only remaining need is getting food. Everything revolves around that quest.

For many of us, the garbage heap near the central kitchen is much more interesting than the Puf. That's where they dump the leftovers, and although it's strictly forbidden even to be in that vicinity, many a person, usually at dusk, attempts to dig up little pieces of turnips or other leftover foods.

Several times such activity has cost somebody his life. One of the higher SS officers from Monowitz, a certain Captain Rackasj, has picked this particular spot as his private hunting ground. Apparently he has killed quite some "game" already. Everybody, including myself, is scared to death of this man.

Every time we leave the camp in the morning, while the orchestra plays its march music, I am relieved. I know I am the exception. Most people are glad to return alive in the evening. But when the door of my little palace closes behind me, I am instantly in a different world. It is an oasis of peace and security. In the morning, at my leisure, I do the necessary work in my palace, and the rest of the time I spend visiting Benno and organizing my business.

We now have a big oat bin in which we store quite a lot of merchandise. Aside from the vodka, we occasionally have ham, cheese, jars of marmalade, and other items for the black market all hidden under the rabbit food.

I don't know how he does it, but Benno's organizational talent seems unlimited. And everything goes effortlessly; with amazing ease, he brings me his merchandise as if by some magic trick. I know he gets almost everything via the civilian workers; maybe Brunja plays a role in it too, but I don't get to know the particulars. Almost daily, at Benno's signal, I take two bottles of vodka into the camp. I'm a nervous wreck every time we approach the gate. I know all too well that smuggling is punishable by death. Only after I have delivered the goods does the tension ease.

One morning, not very long after we started using the oat bin for storage purposes, I notice that a big ham is missing. I don't understand. I always lock the building at night, and only Vraneck and I have a key. I immediately go over to Benno and report the theft. "Vraneck," he says, "only Vraneck could have done this. Don't worry. I'll take care of it." "How do you intend to do that?" I ask. "Who can handle a man like Vraneck in a situation like this?" "Rackasj," Benno answers and looks at me meaningfully.

Then it is quiet. My brain is working like crazy. Slowly but surely I'm getting the picture. It could not be true. I had thought about it before, but it seemed so absurd that I immediately dismissed the thought. But now it is crystal clear: Benno, somehow, has contacts with the feared Rackasj. But of course! Through that friendly SS officer from Latvia.

Instantly, the puzzle fits, but it is a frightening picture. We are servicing the SS with our business. In other words, I'm smuggling for the Krauts! Rackasj and his cronies are drinking the vodka that I risk my life to smuggle into the camp, and they are eating the ham and cheese that have been stored in my oat bin. Why didn't Benno tell me? What do I really know about Benno? Almost nothing. Maybe it is better this way. The less I know, the less vulnerable I am.

Silently, we stand there. He is my teacher, counselor, protector, partner, and friend. Our fates are glued together. I have to trust him; there is no alternative, no turning back. When I look into the oat bin the next morning, the ham is back in its place. How far does Benno's influence reach? I stand in total awe of him.

❖ INGE ❖

—————————————————————

"Get up, get up, fast, faster." It feels like we just got into bed when we're being chased out of our barrack in the middle of the night. Surprise check. In no time we line up in our usual rows of five. Shivering from the night chill and fear, we huddle together. Like always, they're hitting us left, right, and center to get us in line. How could we ever have thought their counting would be just a daytime ritual? Two or three times those present are counted, but it doesn't add up to the number that is supposed to be on the list. That is wrong, very wrong.

One by one, our camp numbers are read, and it soon turns out number such-and-such is missing. We all know him. He is a nice quiet boy, about seventeen. In our barrack, he is known to be the loverboy of the barrack elder of a nearby building. We have been waiting forever when he finally shows up. Bleeding from mouth and nose, he is led into the detention barrack in the gray early morning. He is just a kid. Sobbing loudly and crouching, he passes us. He must have been in bed with his protector when the Germans rushed in.

It is daylight when we finally get back to our straw mattresses. I am wide awake and can't get back to sleep. With my eyes wide open, I stare at the half-dark barrack and keep seeing the kid with his bloody nose. He had looked like a schoolboy who had been in a brawl during the break. He was just a child.

So was Inge Meyerhof. A beautiful little girl with a round face, talking eyes, and light brown hair. In the years before the outbreak of the war, now and then we had had Jewish refugees from Germany in our house. They had all been in transit. Most attempted to escape to America via Dutch harbors. Inge had arrived just before the war, and it had soon become clear that it would be impossible for her to flee any farther westward. The Dutch authorities did not offer any help. On the contrary, Jewish refugees were either sent back at the border or interned in a refugee camp in the village of Westerbork.

So Inge stayed with us. We all were very fond of this happy, un-complicated person who learned to speak Dutch in no time. Kitty, Elly, and I all of a sudden had gotten a younger sister. In the night of October 2, 1942, during a countrywide raid on the Jews, our family got picked up and deported to Westerbork. Inge had been with us. Elly, who had gotten married shortly before that, had been with her in-laws and had therefore escaped.

The day before, I had bumped into "fat Spier," a not-very-well-liked Jewish fellow citizen who lived with his sister close to where we lived. Everybody avoided this heavy-set man who reportedly had ties with the Germans. Spier had come up to me as I was on my way to the city center.

We normally would have just said a perfunctory hello, but this time he had stopped to talk to me. "Listen, Louis," he had said as he furtively looked around, "it is going to happen tonight or tomorrow night. They are going to pick up ninety people, but your family is not on the list." "Are you sure?" I had asked in shock. "Yes, I am," fat Spier had answered. He then proceeded on his way home without any further explanation.

I had rushed back home and told my parents what I had just heard. For a brief moment there had been a light panic. A little while back, a business friend of my father's, a butcher from Grubbenvorst, a certain Mr. Joosten, had offered us a hiding place, but we had not taken him up on it at the time.

What to do? Leave now, or stay? For weeks, our suitcases had been packed and ready to take at a moment's notice. We were prepared for the worst, we thought. "Let's wait for tomorrow," my father had said. "If we're not on the list, we can decide tomorrow at our leisure what is best." That evening, we had gone to bed at ten.

In the middle of the night, a loud and long ringing of the doorbell. We wake up and know immediately what's going on. As I hurry to put on my pants, I hear my father go down the stairs. I realize he must have been sleeping fully dressed. A few seconds later, at the top of the stairs, I see two constables from the Nijmegen police standing in the corridor. In a town like Nijmegen, everybody knows them. Their names are Wiebe and de Ruiter. While we silently get our suitcases together, the two are leisurely smoking cigarettes in our kitchen. They have noticed that Elly is not home. Father has shown them Elly's wedding papers as proof of the reason why she left her parental home. Obviously, he does not tell them she is staying with her in-laws at 33 Hindestraat.

With her red, sleepy cheeks, Inge comes down the steps. Mother has woken her up and dressed her. Shivering in her light blue coat, she is waiting in the corridor. She has put her little checkered suitcase with the dark brown corners between her legs. Rosa, our dog, a boxer who has been her biggest friend since she arrived, stays faithfully at her side. He rubs his warm body against her left leg as if to protect her.

Twenty minutes later, we are in the waiting room of the Nijmegen police station with a number of other arrested Jews. Rosa had been personally taken away by Commissioner van Dijk upon our arrival. Inge's tears and father's and my protests had left him completely unmoved.

At the first light of dawn, from the window of our train compartment, we see the silhouette of Nijmegen diminish rapidly. The tower of St. Steven's Church with the round globe below the weathercock is the last thing we see of our town. Inge is sitting beside me. Pale and quiet, she looks out of the windows. In a protective manner, I put my arm on her shoulder. "Are they going to kill Rosa?" she asks in a very thin voice. "Of course not," I say convincingly, "a beautiful dog like that, no way!"

February 16, 1943, in transit camp Westerbork, they're reading out loud the list of prisoners destined for deportation to Poland. " ...Jacob de Wijze, Sarah de Wijze-Katan, Inge Meyerhof. . ."

Inge's light blue coat dances like a butterfly in the gray crowd near the train. In one hand she carries her suitcase; her other hand holds my mother's. Then, briefly, she turns her head and gives Kitty and me a sweet smile, as if to comfort us.

By Louis de Wijze

❖ Two Bottles ❖
of Vodka

The days are passing. It is summer now. Nobody can remember if we ever had springtime. Many of us have disappeared. One day, Aron and Jankle are gone. Nobody knows their whereabouts.

As the temperature rises, there seems to be more sickness and disease. The sick bay is overflowing, and the trips to the crematoria of Birkenau are on the increase. The lack of even basic medication makes even the most innocent physical inconveniences an unbearable torture.

One day my jaw starts to itch tremendously. It turns out I have phlegmon again. A red, round swelling irritates my skin so badly that I have to see a doctor. But immediately they chase me away. There is no ointment. "You have to apply your own urine," somebody suggests. What? My own urine on my face? No way. But when I ask Benno's advice, he says the same. "Just do it. I've seen it before. It works." For lack of anything better, I follow his advice. To my joy, the swollen, infected area goes down within a few days. Within a week, it is completely gone.

Alongside one of the factory chimneys in the middle of Buna, the authorities have affixed a long cable with a red and white basket at the end. It is a simple early-warning system in case of air strikes. As soon as the Germans receive the message that bombers are on their way, the basket is hoisted about halfway up. Possible strike! Warning! If indeed the planes turn out to be on their way to Buna, the basket is hoisted all the way to the top of the chimney. Air strike!

So far we have not seen any planes. We did see the basket go up halfway several times, but those had been false alarms. In the meantime, most of the damage to the factory has been repaired, and the construction continues at high speed.

On one of those searing hot days at the end of July, about ten in the morning, we hear a thundering noise coming from the carbide factory. It lasts a few seconds, but the sound is so loud that I initially think it's an explosion or an air strike. As I get out of my little palace, I see nothing, no smoke or fire. It's eerily quiet. From all sides, curious people are running toward the factory. I join them.

From afar, we can see what happened. Near the carbide factory is a track used by heavy railroad cars loaded with coke and calcium for the ovens that produce the carbide. While in the factory, I had often watched how, from a height, the ore is poured through a wide opening into a gigantic storage bunker. We don't know exactly what has happened, but we can see that one of the railroad cars has fallen from the slope down into the bunker.

Very early this morning, somebody must have tampered with the technical installations. When the topheavy colossus appeared over the ore bunker, it must have derailed and dropped into the hole. The mess and the damage are incredible. Everybody knows it's going to take days, maybe weeks, before the damage is repaired and production resumes. We wisely stay at a distance, because there are a lot of uniforms about, and a lot of shouting is going on.

At twelve, as I'm standing in the breadline, I hear that a number of prisoners, including the kapo in charge, have been arrested and taken away. Everybody is talking about our next roll call at the courtyard. An act like this can lead to only one result. That very same afternoon, there is a rumor that the Germans are planning to massively avenge the act of sabotage. The tension remains for the rest of the day, but fortunately nothing happens.

At four, I walk to Benno's shed as usual. As I get nearer, I hear some singing coming from the little office. I hesitate for a moment, then I enter. I am watching a very strange scene. Benno and the Latvian SS officer are loudly singing a Russian drinking song as they pass the vodka bottle back and forth.

The moment they notice me in the doorway, they motion me to join them. I smilingly reject the bottle. The Latvian jumps on the shaky wooden table and starts a sort of Cossack dance. He is as drunk as a skunk. Benno claps his hands and sings along. I watch them for a moment, then I turn around and head for the door. Benno steps in front of me but keeps singing. Out of the officer's sight, he gives me a wink to show me he is fully in control of the situation. Then he dances over to the Latvian who, in the meantime, has dropped on the bench with wild and incoherent laughter.

I step outside, thinking about Benno. What did I just witness? Benno had been absolutely sober. What was he up to? Even though I've known him for a while, he remains a mystery. I feel it will always be that way. It will have to do. I have no desire to learn more.

Now and then Benno asks me to smuggle merchandise out of the camp, not into it. It is mostly stuff from new prisoners who have been deported directly to Monowitz. The newcomers have suitcases and bags full of their possessions that are being confiscated immediately upon their arrival.

In charge of the unit that does the "reception" is an incredible brute, a totally unscrupulous man. He is the lover of one of the SS officers and enjoys complete protection. He rules with an iron fist among this chaos of clothes, books, bread, shoes, watches, and other things. Everybody hates him with a passion. People whisper that this devilish man has become a millionaire here in the camp. Nobody knows if this is true. What we do know is that he leads a very luxurious life and has all the protection you can possibly have.

One day a big transport with Hungarian Jews enters Monowitz. It is one of the many shipments from the country of the Danube. The camp is bursting out of its seams. The barracks are totally crammed, and everywhere we hear their incomprehensible language. That very same night, Benno hands me a small Persian rug. Could I smuggle this to Buna tomorrow morning?

Without any doubt, the rug must belong to the Hungarians. Now I know for sure that Benno must either directly or indirectly have connections with the hated "loverboy." How else can he have organized this business so quickly? The more I think about Benno, the more of a mystery he becomes. How well do I know him? What is really behind that friendly smile, that calm, fatherly voice? Why have I, almost from the outset and without hesitation, fully entrusted myself to him? Can I completely trust him? And what about the young Latvian SS officer? What about Rackasj and that disgusting "loverboy"? Can one keep one's integrity when dealing with the scum of the earth?

These questions keep repeating themselves. But each time I dismiss them. Benno is Benno, the only lifeline I have.

The next morning, I take the rug from under my straw bed, wrap it around my naked body, and put my clothes on. It's difficult to walk. My upper legs have limited movement, and the crotch of my pants sits nearly at my knees. I pull the cord around my pants very tight so the rug stays in place. Without any trouble, I deliver the rug in Buna.

When we march back that evening, upon arrival at the gate, our unit is directed to the side. Checkpoint! I'm almost paralyzed with fear because I'm carrying two bottles of vodka. In my head, I'm climbing the steps to the gallows. There's only one punishment for smuggling: hanging.

I'm breaking out in a cold sweat when three SS officers start to walk past the rows. Everybody is searched. Is there anything I can do? Can I hide the bottles somewhere, or drop them without anyone noticing? But I don't get the chance to do anything. They just grab me. I close my eyes, waiting for the explosion. Rapidly the hands go from the armpits, over my sides, hips, legs, down to my clogs. Then they grab my crotch and down my legs, one by one. Then, suddenly, the hands are gone. I just stand there motionless, eyes closed.

Why doesn't anything happen? I open my eyes a little bit. Nothing. The hands are already working on my neighbor. Petrified, I stay there until the danger is moving away from me. What is going on? Why is this check so sloppy, so un-German? Then an absurd thought: Maybe Rackasj knows how the vodka is smuggled in and where the bottles are hidden in the clothes. Maybe he has given special instructions for the search, in order to make sure the bottles would not be found.

As the officers get farther away from me, all of a sudden I start to smell my own sweat. It drips profusely from my face to my neck. My clothes are sticking to my skin. Then the order: "Continue!" Nothing has been found. Later, at the food distribution, my knees are still shaking.

❖ HUGO ❖

It is a very hot evening when our torturers have decided on a second selection since my stay in Monowitz. In those minutes before the grim reapers come to the barracks, the scene is one of complete chaos.

The prisoners are trying everything to look their healthiest and best. Some go as far as beating their own and other prisoners' bodies just to get a nice rosy color. Others are practicing their walk. They straighten their backs, swing their arms like soldiers, and try to keep their heads upright. Even their facial expressions are trained.

In different circumstances, this would have been a ridiculous show, but this is a deadly serious situation. One's life can depend on one move; each impression can be decisive.

A hollow shout, and the judges come in. Despite the heat, we are shivering, and we wait for that nonchalant gesture that beckons our naked bodies to step forward. Diagonally behind me I see Hugo, the mild-mannered Czech, thinner than ever. Naked, he looks so thin that no trick is going to save him from the claws of the selection. Every bit of fat on his body is gone. His skeleton is kept together by a wrinkly, scurvy skin. The weakened muscles have lost most of their functions. It must even hurt him just to sit down because there are only bones where there once was flesh.

Panicky, Hugo looks around in his agony, searching for a way to escape the upcoming verdict. Nobody pays attention to him. Everybody minds his own business. In the midst of the group, he looks like a lone man in the desert. Without making a sound, he screams his fear, but nobody listens. I look at him and feel his pain. In his despair, the misery of us all is reflected. Why don't I avert my face? Why can't I shake this agonizing look? I hardly know him. A nice man, nothing more. I owe him nothing.

My heart pounds in my throat when a hand beckons me. The moment of truth has arrived. I rush forward. So fast have I passed the table with the fatal list, they hardly got the chance to take a good look at me. The heavy weight of the tension immediately drops off me. Taking a deep breath, I walk back in a big circle, take my clothes, and join the others. Nearby, there is still a small group waiting for the beckoning hand. Hugo is the last one.

My eyes go down his rib cage and bony legs. Because his anal muscles are no longer working, his rectum is hanging out of his anus. Suddenly, he turns around. His face reads utter despair, and his eyes are almost popping out of their sockets. He is looking straight at me. His lips are moving as in silent prayer. Then it happens, almost involuntarily. Like a zombie, I walk toward him, hand him my bundle of clothes, and unobtrusively push him out of the line.

For a moment, he is petrified, his face one big question mark. Then he slips away toward those who are already dressed. The last in line, I soon walk past the table-again. I'm oblivious to any surrounding sounds. It's like a swarm of bees inside me buzzing me into a deep sleep. Shivering, I join the others again.

Nobody at the table has noticed my deceit. The number of prisoners that appeared has matched the list. None of the prisoners has seen what I've done either. When the barrack door finally is shut, the tension discharges in a storm of cheers and lamentations. I am not part of it. Silently, I watch them. Then Hugo stands in front of me. He hands me my clothes and cries. He opens his mouth to say something but is unable to get even a single word out. Tears are running down his cheeks. I'm about to touch him, say something nice to him, but I turn around and walk away.

Later, in the dark on my straw bed, my sanity returns. My act of heroism has had no value for Hugo. His suffering has only been extended. Undoubtedly he will soon go through the chimney of Birkenau. I needlessly risked my own life. For a brief moment, I allowed myself to be guided by feelings from a previous life, feelings that I did not know still existed.

A few weeks later, on a bright, sunny morning, I notice that Hugo's bed is being slept on by another prisoner. I never find out when and how Hugo disappeared. In the distance, as on every day, a plume of smoke rises over the skies of Birkenau.

By Louis de Wijze

❖ New Air Strikes ❖

August 1944. Attack! No sooner have we seen the basket at the top of the chimney then the first bombs are dropped. I instinctively rush out of my little palace. Before I know it, I'm getting carried into a maelstrom of people. In blind panic, the masses run around. Blinded and suffocated by the smoke and dust, I'm making my way toward the light and fresh air.

Chased by death, we run in between the factory halls, away from the fire and flying debris. Then suddenly we are thrown to the ground by air pressure from an explosion to the right of us. The central power station has been hit. Bull's-eye! I get up, unhurt, and start to run like a maniac. For maybe fifteen minutes I go full speed until I almost pass out. Totally out of breath, I reach the electric fence on the north side of Buna. In a daze, I see dozens of prisoners and civilians scaling the fence and jumping off on the other side. What about the electric current? But of course the central generator has been hit.

In no time, I too am on the other side. I keep going. Running, stumbling, and sometimes creeping, we are getting away from the fiery hell behind us. For at least another half hour, we torture our weakened bodies in our hasty flight from death. But then, from one second to the next, my legs refuse. I'm pulling myself on a little mound and drop facedown in a trench. I cannot go another yard. I lie down and throw up, totally exhausted. When the thunder has stopped and our plagued bodies have rested a bit, we slowly get up.

In the distance, black clouds are rising to the sky. We look at one another. Our hair is white from all the dust, and our faces, covered with soot, more than ever look like skulls. From all sides, we flock together. Here we are. No electric wire to hold us, no locks to keep us imprisoned. The landscape of summer dances around us. A happily chirping lark climbs to the sky. For minutes we are basking in the warm sun. A rainbow of colors fills our teary eyes, and our nostrils are savoring the summer herbs. Close by, someone squats down and, like a child on the beach, lets the dry sand run between his fingers.

Everywhere in the green fields, silhouettes of escapees start to appear. There is a lot of talking and shouting. Indecisively, we walk back and forth. Slowly but surely, group after group starts to move back in the direction of Buna. For a moment, I hesitate. Far in the distance, I see a small church tower. Poland and then Germany. I wouldn't stand a chance. Better to go back to the barracks. Very tired, I join the column back to Buna.

To think that imprisonment and comfort could be one and the same . . .

After the air strike, Buna is badly damaged. The fire has been extinguished, but for days the debris keeps smoldering, and we can smell the penetrating stench of fire in a wide area. Again, dozens of casualties. In the midst of the smoldering ruins, I find my little palace unharmed. All the rabbits have survived the catastrophe.

For days, the air strikes are the topic of conversation. Even though the consequences are horrendous, the survivors have been given hope. The Allies are on their way. We know that every bomb brings us closer to them.

Again the rumor goes, as after the first bombardment, that secret agents have infiltrated Buna, giving the Allies information as to the best timing of the air strikes. Where the rumors originate and whether they are true, nobody knows. But it is a fact that the bombardments seem to take place when the construction reaches an important final stage. Coincidence? We don't know, but we are keeping hope alive by fiercely upholding the rumor.

The day after the air strikes, I meet Robert Wiggins during the lunch break at our regular spot. He looks distressed. With tears in his eyes, he tells me a number of bombs hit the English stalag. His friend Jimmy did not have to work at Buna that day but had to do a job at the POW camp. One of the bombs hit the building Jimmy just happened to be in. Shattered, Robert stands in front of me. He face shows big black bags under his eyes. The loss of his friend has affected him tremendously. When he walks away, he suddenly is an old man.

The bombs and the fire have paralyzed almost all vital sections of Buna. Some of the buildings are completely destroyed; others are severely damaged. Gigantic mounds of debris, with the steel skeletons still intact here and there, are making the factory site look even sadder. Unlike after the first bombardments, the Germans decide to postpone the reconstruction. Priority now goes to the building of bunkers.

First things first. Of course, the bunkers are for the Germans and civilian workers only. It is unthinkable that Jews or other "subhumans" would take refuge in them. On the contrary, at the next strike, we are ordered to stay on the site. Anyone who doesn't will be summarily executed, probably because a number of Polish prisoners did manage to escape after the last bombardment. Even though the Germans searched the area with dogs for hours, the fugitives have not been found.

In the following days, almost all units are put to work removing debris and clearing the factory site. The one thing that has priority is the repair of the central power station.

Even though we are encouraged by the air strikes and have gotten some hope for a quick and favorable end to the war, nothing changes as far as our circumstances are concerned. On the contrary, it feels as if the cruelty of our torturers has increased, and they have to take out their anger and frustration on us. More than ever, they kick and beat us, yell and scream, and shoot prisoners for the slightest offense.

More and more often, we witness some hopeless victim hanging in the six thousand-volt fence; more and more frequently, people are taking their belts and hanging themselves in the barracks at night. Fortunately, none of the victims is someone I know.

Sometimes we hear the faraway, muffled thunder from the Russian front. Regularly we can hear explosions emanating from the Carpathian Mountains where Polish partisans are assailing the hated oppressor time and again.

We know the Germans at the Eastern front are fleeing, and the Allies are now making good advances in the west. Everybody is talking about an imminent, total collapse of the Third Reich. But how much time do we have? There is great fear that we won't make it to liberation. Every day that we manage to stay alive is a bonus. Nothing is certain but the unpredictability of our torturers. We're alive only by the grace of fate, the luck of the moment.

In the midst of all this misery, my own existence at Buna still has a silver lining. It is absurd that I can peacefully do my job as a rabbit caretaker and contraband smuggler for the Krauts. Sometimes I think that somewhere in the universe my fate has been predestined, having crossed the path of people like Herbert, Benno, and Vraneck.

In less than two weeks, planes reappear on the horizon. Soon the basket appears at the top of the chimney. As we dash, with pounding hearts, to the faraway corners of Buna, the Germans are, both inside and outside the fence, opening big sulfur-filled canisters. Within a few minutes, the entire area is filled with a yellow, poisonous mist in order to obscure the factory from the approaching planes. The horrendous smoke takes our breath away and causes an unbearable irritation to our eyes. Puking and coughing, we look for a safe place. We hide behind a big heap of coal, close to an antiaircraft gun manned by two young Germans.

Then the bombs drop. For long minutes at a time the sky above our heads thunders and shakes the earth like a wounded animal. Scared to death and defenseless, we lie on the sooted soil, arms folded over our heads.

During a few seconds of relative peace, I look at the silent piece of artillery and see that the young boys have left their posts. Not far away, they're huddling together, sobbing and shivering. The moment a plane dives down to attack, they run away in panic. Their much-too-large helmets are bobbing on their heads. How old could they be? Sixteen at most. Far from their parental home, they run for their young lives.

When the planes have gone and the sulfurous cloud has risen, we return to our work sites. This time, there are fewer victims, and the damage is less than before, but it is clear to everyone that Buna has been crippled for good. But again, my little palace has withstood the tornado.

❖ FRIED CHICKEN ❖

It is only November when the entire Polish landscape is covered in snow. Life is paralyzed by an icy cold. The German murder machine has got itself another ally: winter.

Our ranks are rapidly getting thinner. The first victims of the bitter cold are from Mediterranean countries. Not used to this extreme weather, they fall like flies, dozens at a time. But the death rate among the Dutch, the Belgians, and the French is rising rapidly, too.

We have not had any selections for a while; they are no longer necessary. The weaker ones are just dying more quickly. Only the strong, the sly, and the privileged can survive these exceptional circumstances.

Thanks to my tobacco trade and vodka smuggling, my physical condition, compared to that of most others, is reasonably good. Of course, I too have lost weight, but the extra calories enable me to fend off the wasting cold and the contagious diseases all around. The fact that I am still spared the hard labor in the building units is, of course, invaluable. Under the auspices of Vraneck, I am allowed to continue taking care of the rabbits.

Recently he has been coming in every so often with a big burlap sack and taking a few well-fed animals, but fortunately I can continue my job. I cherish my animals and guard them like a hen guards her chicks. They are my term life insurance.

In the middle of December, early one morning, Vraneck calls us together. He needs four men. His eyes are scouting the lines. It never fails: I am selected as one of the four. We do not like these sudden changes. They are usually bad news.

"You are honored to shovel snow at Dr. Hinder's office this morning," he says with a mocking voice. Relieved, we breathe again. It could have been much worse. Armed with shovels and brooms, we follow him. It no longer snows, but the cold cuts through our thin clothing. Vraneck takes us to our destination, gives us the necessary instructions, and disappears quickly.

We take a relaxed look at the site. Aside from the path to the office, we have to shovel and sweep up everything around it. The snow is about twenty inches deep, and it's harder than we think. But we have learned "to work with our eyes," and besides, it is very early. For now, there is no one to watch us. Easy does it.

We make sure we work hard enough not to die from the cold. Meanwhile, we exchange the latest news and speculate about the end of the war. This goes on for a few hours when, all of a sudden, the door of the office opens and Hinder steps out. We jump up. Has he been inside all this time?

He is standing right in front of me, on the doorstep. A small man, he almost looks ridiculous in his knickerbockers. Out of habit, I immediately step aside to let him through, but Hinder does not move. With an ice-cold look, he evaluates the situation. His fat face with the round spectacles slowly turns from one prisoner to the next. We feel something coming.

"Goddamn shit Jews," he erupts with a high-pitched hoarse voice. Then he takes two steps forward, and with one kick, knocks me off my feet. Shovel and all, I smash to the ground. "You call that work? Lazy pigs, vermin!"

With an abrupt move, he yanks a little whip out of one of his boots and lashes out, fiercely, at the face of one of the others. "If this place is not swept squeaky clean within the hour, I'll have all four of you shipped to Birkenau, today!" he yells, his face now purple. "Understood? What the hell do you think, you scurvy dogs, you impudent, dirty pigs!"

Frantically, we start to shovel and sweep. But just as he appeared, he disappears between the factory buildings. Without allowing ourselves any rest, we keep working. We are so afraid we don't even dare talk to one another. In no time, the job is done. Quickly, we make sure we have not forgotten anything. Then we get the hell out of there. With a sigh of relief, I arrive at my little palace.

A few days before Christmas, the rumor goes that the Germans have launched a counterattack at the Western front. We hear that the Allies have suffered heavy losses at the hands of the Germans in the Belgian Ardennes. Vraneck brings me this news personally.

One morning he suddenly shows up at my palace. "Dutchman, have you heard the news?" he blurts out triumphantly. "Within a few days, we will be back in Antwerp. The tide has turned in our favor. The final victory is ours. Like I've always said, when push comes to shove, the German armies are invincible!" He babbles on, beaming.

In a theatrical pose, he gazes out of the little round windows at the gray winter sky, hands on his hips. It has not occurred to him that he is there with somebody else who is able to form his own opinion. I'm just decor, a piece of the furniture. I am just there for him to dispel his old insecurity and to talk himself back into self-assuredness and courage.

He walks to the hutches and lifts one of the rabbits by the scruff of his neck, going on and on. "We've got them, Dutchman. Soon there will be nothing left of them. We'll drive them all back into the North Sea!" I remain silent. Not a word passes my lips. Suddenly, he stops his speech. He looks at me and ponders aloud, as if only now aware of my presence.

"It is even better for you Jews that we win the war," he says, stroking his chin. "Who knows, all of you may be allowed to migrate to Madagascar." Then, jocular laughter, and he is off, head tilted backward, chin in the air, as if the final victory has already been achieved and the parades have started.

The unexpected German successes are a big damper on our already weakened mental defenses. Thus far, we had heard only of the advancing Russian troops, of the ever-increasing bombardments of German cities, and of the liberation of Belgium and the south of the Netherlands. In one fell swoop, all our hopes are dashed. Could the Krauts still turn the tide? Depressed, I go to visit Benno. With a smile he listens to my lamentations.

"Just think," he says in a fatherly tone, "the Krauts have to defend themselves on two gigantic fronts. You don't believe in miracles, do you? No, don't worry, it is over for them, very soon. I can assure you." That was it. He then immediately changes the topic and tells me he is going to be in a Christmas show in the camp.

In an unheard-of show of magnanimity, the Germans have given the okay, just this once, for the organization of an evening of theater. It will take place in one of the "prominent" barracks and will be performed by and for the prisoners. Unfortunately, the show will be for a limited audience. Only the "prominent" will have access to this culture fest.

"You'll never guess what imitation I'm going to do," Benno says with a sparkle in his eyes. "Charlie Chaplin!" He begins the famous duckwalk, feet turned outward, swinging his walking stick, and greeting with his bowler hat. It is a very funny sight. Too bad I won't be able to watch Benno display his talent onstage.

In the dusky room, we ponder the upcoming holidays and think about the good old days. "Do you know what I did for Christmas two years ago?" I ask. I tell him how the entire German elite had celebrated their yule fest at the house of Camp Commander Gemmeker in Westerbork. December 19, 1942.

At the time, I, along with some other young Jews, had been a messenger for the Germans. We took care of the communications in the camp and delivered messages, more or less doing their little chores. The day of the yule fest itself, Gemmeker had sent us to get haircuts. We had to look pristine, because he had something nice in mind for "his boys."

That night we had lined up, neatly dressed and crisply cut, outside the commander's building. As the gleaming automobiles with the elite had arrived, we had jumped forward, courteously helping the ladies out of their cars, gallantly offering them our arms and accompanying them inside in a stately manner.

"Would you believe I personally offered my arm to Miss Winkelkamper, secretary to SS Colonel Ausder Funten? I can still smell her perfume!"

As Benno listens intently, I tell him about my stay at Camp Westerbork. How rich cultured life really was back there. There were shows, beautiful concerts. Famous Jewish names from the world of music and theater had performed onstage: Max Ehrlich, Willy Rosen, Camilla Spira, Gunther Witebski, and many others. The Germans had sat in the first row and enjoyed the show and applauded.

When I finish my story, it is quiet for a while. Darkness has set in. "You think they're still alive?" I ask. Almost un-noticeably, Benno shrugs. His fingers are tapping softly on the simple wooden table.

Christmas has passed. The show must have been a tremendous success. Everybody who has seen it is still talking about it. The Germans had even arranged the requisite stage costumes. Benno has instantly become famous. Everybody calls him Charlie.

To our amazement, we receive white bread and sausages on Christmas Day. The soup that night is the most nutritious ever, thick and filled with bits of potatoes and even some meat here and there. Are the Germans becoming sentimental because it was Christmas? Do they feel a little guilty? Has the sound of the ever-approaching guns played a role in this? We do not know and do not want to know. We greedily gulp up our ration. What's in your stomach is in. Tomorrow is another day. We'll worry about that then.

The last afternoon of the year, I am not in my little palace but in the carbide factory, together with Elkan Speyer. I have known him for about two months. He is from Leeuwarden in the north of Holland. His hair is dark blond and he has blue eyes; he looks very Frisian to me. Except for a big nose, he does not look Jewish at all. He radiates a natural calm, even more so than Benno.

The first time we met had been after a soccer game. His warm personality had stood out. Just like Benno, Elkan knows the art of survival, but of all the people I have got to know here at Buna and back in the camp, he is by far the most sociable. He will share his last piece of bread, that little bit of marmalade, and even half a cigarette with his friends. It makes him a very special human being.

"Listen, Louis," he had said this morning as we marched through the gate, "how about celebrating New Year's Eve this afternoon, you and I? Come over to the carbide factory after the lunch break, and we'll have a little party."

At the agreed time, Elkan waited for me at the entrance and took me to a dark, deserted corner of the factory. In amazement, I watch him take a roasted chicken, wrapped in a greasy paper, from under his clothes. And not even a small chicken!

"What do you think?" he asks with glimmering eyes as he breaks off a leg and hands it to me. Tears fill my eyes. For a moment, I am speechless. A feeling of happiness pervades me. "That is so wonderful of you," I reply with a suddenly hoarse voice.

Elkan smiles at me. Then he picks up an imaginary glass and makes a toast. *"L'chaim,* Louis. Here is to the New Year." *"L'chaim"* I say, "Here is to your health." Simultaneously we empty our invisible glasses with one gulp and attack our delicious meal. A real meal! We pick the carcass clean, to the last little bone.

❖ Exodus ❖

Evacuation. Word spreads through the camp. It is January 17, and we have returned from Buna earlier than normal.

It looks like an anthill that has just been disturbed by an anteater. There is only one topic: The Russians are coming! There is a nervous tension everywhere.

But not only the prisoners look agitated and panicky. The Germans, too, seem to be close to a mental collapse. They are running all over the place, trying to move boxes and chests. Motorbikes are racing back and forth.

Russians! That one word seems to drive the Germans to a frenzy. There is nothing left of that arrogance that prevailed after the start of the Ardennes counteroffensive. For days their faces have been somber and pale. They know it. All of them know it. It has gone wrong, completely wrong. The Russians are coming.

"Tomorrow night the camp will be evacuated," Benno tells me after his return from his daily reporting. Everyone who is able to walk has to come along. Only the sick can stay. "Don't you believe that for a moment," somebody shouts. "You can bet that everybody who stays behind will be killed."

"Where are we going?" I ask Benno.

"I don't know, but we are going to have to walk because the railroad no longer works," he says in a somber voice.

That last night, we pack the few things we own. Some have managed to organize some extra clothes. I don't have to do much. Except for my plate and spoon, the handle of which I have sharpened into a knife, I take only some bread rations. My clothes are complete. My clog shoes are in reasonable shape.

Our last night in Monowitz is bitter cold. Shivering, we lie on our straw sacks. Tomorrow it is going to happen. But where to? How far? Suppose the Russians arrive here tonight? Are the Germans going to keep us alive, or will they shoot us anyway? Dozens of questions keep dancing in my head. I toss and turn in the dark. On foot, through this harsh, wintry country-how long would we survive such a thing in our physical condition? One thing I know for sure: Everybody who stays behind has had it. With my head full of awful premonitions, I manage to fall asleep.

Very late the next afternoon, we start our march and leave the courtyard. Block by block receives the command to get moving. It is almost completely dark. The searchlights on the watchtowers are still doing their job, shining their light over the barracks and the area. *arbeit macht frei.* For the last time, the text bespatters us.

It is as if the snow has been waiting for us. Barely through the gate, the snowflakes suddenly start falling by the millions from the dark sky.

Guarded on both sides by heavily armed and warmly dressed SS officers, we walk into the night. Our clogs are crunching on the snowy street, echoing thousands of times. The cold that already stiffened our muscles in the courtyard now slowly but surely starts to pervade our entire bodies. Hunching our bodies over, we continue.

Although we leave barrack by barrack, there soon is no order whatsoever left in this long line. The slower ones fall back. I manage to keep up with the tempo. I'm passing more and more people. Far behind us, we hear a gunshot every now and again.

Someone next to me stumbles and bumps into someone else. "Watch it, go on, man! Can't you hear those shots? If you stay behind, you die! Do you want to be shot in the neck as well?" The little Frenchman curses like a madman but then helps the other man back onto his feet.

My legs are starting to hurt. How long have we been walking? Where is Benno? I look around me. We are like a long winding river, moaning and groaning everywhere. More and more, I hear the sound of executions in the back of the line. Directly in front of me, a man tumbles to the outside of the line. Then he lowers himself in the snow. He is giving up. Two SS officers rush toward him and pull him to a ditch alongside the road; one of them puts his pistol against the back of his head. A flame, a resounding thunder in the dark. We continue.

Groups of Ukrainian SS are marching past us. "Hurry. The Russians are close now!" they shout. More and more fugitives are rushing by. Soldiers on horse-drawn carts are galloping like the devil is right on their tails. Passing motorbikes make the snow fly up in the air.

Suddenly, there is a child next to me. I know the little Hungarian fellow. He had been in the barrack next to mine since the summer. He is not much older than ten; without a doubt the youngest person in Monowitz.

He was, of course, a mistake, a weird twist of fate. Probably ended up here through a small error in the German administrative system. His youth had evoked a feeling of tenderness in us. In his barrack, he became a glimmer of hope, a sign, however small, that there was a chance to survive. The people in his barrack cuddled and loved him. Silently, he walks on.

I look at his emaciated body. He is like a little nocturnal animal. Big black eyes in a pointed face. His cap is tightened in the back with a little string in order to fit his tiny head. Unlike us, he has normal shoes, probably the ones he wore when he left home. I don't know why, but I stay next to him. Courageously, he swings his arms. Now and then he looks up at me.

As time goes by, he starts to slow down. His little back is starting to curve more and more. His arms are moving stiffly now alongside his body. His breathing becomes irregular. I reach out my hand to him. For a moment he hesitates, then he puts his bony fist in mine. His fingers are ice-cold. Thus we continue, like a big and small brother.

The snow has settled on our clothes in a thick layer. When at one point he looks at me, I point to myself and say "Louis." Then I point at him: "What's your name?" Without any expression, he looks back at me. Did he understand me? "Piszta," his child voice says, cutting through the freezing air like a knife. That's all he says. Whatever I ask him next, there is no reaction.

Hand in hand, we continue, two strangers. Endlessly we move our legs. How many hours now? Somebody steps on my heel. "Damn it, can't you watch out?" I growl, looking back. The little hand is still in my hand. I'm pulling Piszta along. Don't stop. In the back, there is death. How much longer, how much farther? We shuffle on, hypnotized. We are floating along in the masses, our feet painful, our joints stiff.

Then, as if he just fell from the sky, a familiar figure is next to me. Benno. He taps me on the shoulder. We glance at each other. That's enough. As if I have been reinvigorated. Together again. Silently, we trudge along.

"We are going to Gleiwitz," Benno suddenly says. "I've heard it from a bike rider." It does not mean a thing to me. The only thing that's important is, how far is it? But Benno does not know either.

Little Piszta walks in between us now, still holding my hand. My legs are dead tired. All my muscles ache from attempting to keep my balance on this slippery road. Left, right, left, right, I silently encourage myself.

We have to take a break sometime. The Germans themselves have got to get tired, too. All of a sudden, the sound of thousands of clogs changes. It seems more determined, more penetrating. Contours of houses appear around us. We are marching through a village. The sounds of our wooden shoes bounce off the stone fronts of the houses. No lights, no movements anywhere. Not a glimmer of life in this godforsaken place.

Our guards have posted themselves between the houses. They watch us carefully, their fingers on the triggers, dogs on the leads. They are ready. But who of us could go anywhere? No one, at this point, could do much more than trudge on. Once we are past the houses, the echo disappears.

In the dusk, between dream and reality, we stumble on, mile after mile, in an empty, dark world. It feels as if it has been snowing all our lives. Behind us, the dark sky lights up just as it does with an approaching thunderstorm, followed, seconds later, by the distant noise of guns. Someone says, "The Russians have broken through."

Elkan has joined us now. All of a sudden I see him in front of us, dragging a comrade. Despite being exhausted, we immediately help him. The weight of the man is heavy on our shoulders. Finally he loses consciousness, and we have to leave him behind on the roadside.

Endlessly, we keep on walking. Our lips are chapped, our throats raw. With our blue hands, we scoop the snow from our clothes and gulp it down. What time is it? Is it getting light yet? Now and then I catch a glimpse of a familiar face. Sometimes I can think of the name that goes with it, sometimes not. In this long, icy line, it is everyone for himself. We walk for our lives. If you don't walk, you are dead. Gone is the hierarchy. To belong to the prominent is just a vague memory. It's back to zero. Everybody suffers the same way. The reaper does his work without any distinction.

The snow has stopped. The sky is clear now, and we can see the twinkling stars. It is getting colder, and tears on our faces are starting to freeze. Then a command. Did we hear that correctly? For hours we have begged and screamed for it. Now that we hear it, we don't know how quickly we can go to the side of the road. Take a break.

We race to sit down. People are dropping in the snow, trampled by the pushing crowd. Chaos all around. Near a gate-I can hardly believe my eyes-the Germans are lined up with baskets. If one manages to get near, one gets thrown a piece of bread. The scene is horrific. With foaming mouths, the starved attack one another, hitting, kicking, and biting everyone around them.

Miraculously, all four of us manage to get a piece of bread. We quickly leave the scene. Suddenly I notice that Piszta's little fingers have slipped out of my hand. He has disappeared in the all-absorbing masses.

"Come along," Benno shouts at Elkan and me. Together we push and punch ourselves forward. We now see that we have arrived at the ruins of a brickyard. Hundreds at a time are trying to get inside. There is screaming, crying, and cursing. Everybody wants a place just to drop down and rest, if only for a little while. In the dark, we step on bodies. There is moaning and groaning everywhere.

"This is never going to work," Elkan shouts from the crowd. "Let's go that way." He points toward the dark. We barely manage to wrestle free and hurry in the indicated direction. Under a semi-collapsed roof of one of the drying rooms, we find a few planks to sit on. We huddle together, out of the wind, as much as possible. Others are trying to push us away, but we fiercely defend our turf. Exhausted, we lean against one another, broken and cold. Again, I feel hands pushing me from behind. I turn around to start yet another fight.

"Louis," a little voice sounds beside me. It's Piszta. He must have kept an eye on us at all times. I pull him, shivering like a leaf, onto the plank. "Come, sit here between us." Benno and Elkan immediately make room. We put the little fellow, who is chilled to the bone, in between our protective bodies.

In the dim light of the stars, I look at his ashen face. His eyes half closed, he looks at me, and for the first time I seem to see a faint smile on his lips. Then he just falls asleep. "We have to keep him warm." These caring words come from-who else?-Elkan. Like a ring of trees, we form a protection around the little Hungarian. In turn, we massage and rub his hands and legs. Unaware of it all, the boy sleeps deeply. He doesn't feel a thing. He would have slid peacefully to his death.

We take turns rubbing him in order to stay awake and prevent us from being overcome by the freezing cold. Around us, the sounds are fading. Death strikes without a sound. In his soft and sweet voice, he prods the dead tired to rest their tortured bodies. "Why don't you lie down in that nice, soft, blanket of snow," he tempts. "Nothing could be finer than a deep sleep. Just lie down for a while. A few minutes' rest will do you good."

Shouts. Gather for departure! In a daze, we look around. How long have we sat here? An hour? Half a night? Stiff and incredibly tired, all four of us get up. Close by, an old man is shaking the arm of his lifeless son. "Come on, David, wake up, we have to go. Come on, my boy, please get up!" Unable to understand that his son is no longer with us, he keeps talking to him.

Then Benno walks over to him. "Come on, your son is taken out of his suffering. His pain is over. Come with us," he says in Yiddish and softly takes this broken man by the hand.

We start to walk toward the street, falling and climbing over the frozen corpses. Dozens and dozens of our comrades have fallen victim to the silent pact between sleep and cold. The ever-falling snowflakes will cover them in a white shroud in no time, but there won't be any grave for them. So many dead, but we don't feel any sorrow. Automatically, the shouting gets us moving again.

Step by step, slower and slower, we push our bodies over the white roads. Hour after hour. Nobody has any concept of time, distance, or place. The pain and the cold seem to lift us above ourselves. As if in a trance, we move our feet and keep our bodies upright. Sometimes we wake up, startled. As we were walking, the sleep had surprised us.

It has gotten quiet in the back. The Germans can save their ammunition. The blistering cold and the exhaustion are doing their job now. One after the other, prisoners are dropping in the virgin snow alongside the road, without a sound.

Now and then SS officers zoom by on their motorbikes. Are they announcing our arrival in Gleiwitz? Are the barracks being readied for our arrival?

The guards who accompany us no longer seem as threatening as at the beginning of our march. Now and again they encourage us: "We are almost there." What does that mean, "almost"? It does not seem to end. The horizon remains unreachable. Does Gleiwitz really exist? Are they pulling our legs? We keep walking within one another's sight, little Piszta, Benno, Elkan, and I. Helping others is no longer a consideration. Everybody is busy with his own self. More than busy. The road is endless. Left, right, left, right. . .

It is dark again. Are we still not there? Do we have to spend another night outside? Again we fill our stomachs with snow. At least we quench our thirst. For hours we keep walking. Then suddenly, barbed wire. Gleiwitz!

Like a flash flood, we enter the camp. It is pitch dark, not a light in sight. In this total chaos, we lose Elkan. Benno and I, followed by Piszta, are fighting our way into the barrack. The corridor in between the dormitories is a complete battlefield. We manage to open a door. "Full! Get away! No more space! Get away!" Whatever we do, and however we push, we can't get in. With an angry thud, the door shuts.

With everything that is still left in us, we wrestle back to the corridor. Yard for yard, we advance until we finally manage to reach a corner. Panting from our efforts, we are pressed together. The fatigue makes our legs tremble. Our bodies scream for a place to rest, but it is impossible to sit down. Standing up straight and surrounded by an incredible stench, we are forced to wait for the morning.

Elbows are pushing me in the dark, shoulders are pushing me back and forth. Piszta has lowered himself between us. His hands wrapped around my legs, he sits on the cold floor, wedged in between a forest of legs and clogs.

Completely exhausted, we hang against one another. If only we could lie down for a bit. The floor is so close but so unreachable. I doze off a little bit, then get startled by a push, a sudden move. Again, sleep sucks me out of the pain.

By Louis de Wijze

❖ THE MIRACLE ❖
OF OLOMOUC

Very early in the morning, we get chased out of the barrack, exhausted and stiff. Stumbling and cursing and falling over one another, we go outside. In this first daylight, a bizarre world awaits us.

We are flabbergasted by the scene. Like wax statues, frozen people are sitting and standing between the barracks. Dozens of others are lying still on the ground, covered with a layer of snow. I am looking at their blue, frozen faces. Some of them I recognize from the journey.

Just like us, they had tried to get inside to lay their weary bodies to rest. They had not managed to conquer a spot. In utter despair, they had sought protection between the barracks, but in the black hours of the winter night, death had put his icy fingers on their heads.

"Hurry up, you lazy pigs! Go on! What are you looking at?" We are driven to an open spot. Frightened, Benno, Piszta, and I stay close together. "Have you seen Elkan anywhere?" I ask Benno, who is a little taller than I. Standing on our toes and stretching our necks, we peer through the snowflakes but do not see him anywhere in the gray masses. We wait for hours. Again we are counted, moved about, and counted again. Finally, in the afternoon, the command we have been waiting for: "March!"

The crowd starts to march off the campsite. We worry. Another march on foot? Please don't do this to us, we are praying. We won't make it this time. But less than half an hour later, we stop. Right in front of us, in the middle of this white landscape, is a little railway station. A big, steaming locomotive with a bunch of open railroad cars is waiting. With a lot of noise, the line is subdivided into groups of one hundred and directed to the cars. We get into the designated car, and I rush to a corner. The car fills up very quickly.

We are packed like sardines. The sides of the open car are about chest high. The floor is covered with a thin, trampled layer of snow. Do we really have to travel in this thing?

Two Germans with a pushcart are walking past the train. They are starting to throw loaves into the cars. "One, two, three, four, five, six, seven," we count out loud with them. Seven loaves of bread for a hundred prisoners! The same number of packages of margarine follow. We are getting restless. Our mouths are watering.

When they arrive at our car and the loaves land in our midst, all hell breaks loose. Worse than vultures and hyenas, we dash to the floor. We stumble over one another, cursing and growling. Many minutes later it gets quiet again. Two people are dead on the floor. Empty-handed, I stand in my corner. Not a crumb, not a gram of margarine.

Four SS officers climb into the car, warmly dressed, guns at the ready. They are a little older, their faces marked by time. They position themselves on the floor against the back wall. Around them, prisoners are shrinking back and pressing the others even closer together.

At the order of the guards, we throw the dead onto the platform. The whistle sounds. Haltingly, the train starts to move. It is January 20, 1945, and still snowing.

The train moves slowly through a white, glazy world. Sometimes we stop at a small hamlet for a while, for no apparent reason. Then we continue for a while and stop again. Ride and stop. Snow, snow, never-ending snow. Like white flour bags, we hang against one another. Hours pass. Darkness starts to cover the countryside. For how long can you stand upright? For how long can you do this, packed with almost a hundred people on a small surface, in a severe frost, with snowstorms, with not enough clothes, hungry and thirsty?

Now and then, from pure exhaustion, we slip into a brief sleep. Standing upright, we drift between dream and reality. The cruel shocks of the train ride call us back. Stop, go, stop, go.

In the meantime, the SS officers have been relieved. To my left, there is a short struggle. Somebody pushes me. "It's me, Benno!" In the dark, we are pressed against one another like lovers in an attempt to dispel the cold. This is how we stand, suspended in time, in a still fight against death. Finally the darkness disappears. In a daze, we look around. Who is still alive? We are touching the white snowmen and shaking them. Are they asleep? Are they dead? A little farther down in the car, a corpse is thrown out. Then another, and another.

Suddenly, behind Benno, two dark eyes appear from under a much too large cap. Piszta has made it to the new day. Wedged between a dying man and Benno, he managed to survive. "Come and help me," Benno says.

Together we grab his neighbor who is frozen and leaning against him. We take his coat and pants, and drop him over the edge. The same happens with three other corpses. We put their clothes over our own. Piszta also has an extra coat now, which covers him completely. He is still not speaking a word. From the first day he spent with us, we have been unable to detect any emotion in his taut, little face. Go, stop, go, stop.

Somebody passes a plate. It is filled with watery excrement and urine. It's not the first time. I throw the contents over the edge of the car and hand the plate back to the owner. No doubt he will try to clean it with snow from his clothes.

Aside from the bitter cold, thirst is our worst enemy. Our throats and mouths are dried out and feel like sandpaper. We are scooping some snow with our plates, which are tied to the rope that holds up our pants. The snow is mingled with coal dust, but we don't care and greedily bring it to our mouths. Now and then we sit down, which is now possible because our numbers are shrinking. We have not counted, but at least fifteen bodies have been thrown off our car. But soon we get up again because the danger of freezing to death is too great. Upright, we stomp our feet and swing our arms. Stop and go, stop and go.

Another night. It is no longer snowing. We look up. The stars are starting to appear. A bluish light shines on us. An almost heavenly glow appears on our faces as we look at the sky. Have we ever had a colder night in our lives?

The Germans sit and watch our misery. Under thick, woollen blankets, in warm, fur-lined coats, they see us suffer. They are drinking vodka, eating overstuffed sandwiches, and sometimes singing dirty songs. In the middle of the night, one of us starts to shout, as if gone mad, until his vocal cords become hoarse. Others are taking over. The entire car joins in this powerless protest against a heaven that allows so much suffering. Our guards let us shout. They don't care. They're looking at their watches and counting the hours until they will be relieved.

Again we have slipped into a new day. What day? Who are we? Where do we come from? The name of a place appears on the side: Olomouc. Fifty yards from the platform, we stop. The SS with their ever-present Alsatians walk alongside the train. Do I hear correctly? "Go get bread! Five volunteers per car. Quick!"

In a second, I have climbed off the car with four others. I stand in line, dizzy. Flanked by the SS, we march toward the platform, our legs hurting and our muscles stiff. We have to wait. The loaves of bread still have to be loaded off the truck.

The SS officers are chatting at a distance. My back is leaning against a stack of cardboard boxes. I carefully get my spoon/knife out of my pocket and thrust it deeply into the box behind my back. Slowly, I make a few big incisions. Nobody notices anything.

My hand slips into the box. It cannot be true! I sneak a look around. Holy cow! Very fast, but very carefully, I grab everything I can and put it into my pockets and under my clothes. Not for a moment do I lose sight of the guards. Inside, I'm bubbling over, exhilarated.

Feverishly, I continue. Sugar cubes, little packs of spread-able cheese, rolls of biscuits, chocolate bars, margarine, everything magically disappears into my clothes. Both of my neighbors notice what's going on. They're poking me: What about us? I shuffle away from the boxes. I can't take any more anyway.

A few minutes later, each of us walks back to the train with five loaves under his arms. Twenty-five loaves per car! That's a lot better than in Gleiwitz. We climb back in. This time our guards are keeping the hungry crowd at bay with their rifles. We break the loaves in half and throw the pieces from behind the guards into the famished crowd. With half a loaf under my coat, I make my way toward my corner.

Benno has saved my spot. I quickly hand him the bread. Shivering from all my pent-up emotion, I whisper my secret into his ear. He looks at me as if he has just seen a ghost. "You must be joking," he says in disbelief. "Is that really true?" I nod and bite my lips. "Wait until it is dark," I whisper. We turn our backs to the others, way in the corner of the car.

Unnoticed, I have handed Benno and Piszta a few sugar cubes. Never have we tasted anything more delicious. Under cover of darkness, Benno and I split the loot and hide everything under our clothes. We give Piszta some chocolate, a piece of cheese, and a few biscuits for the night. He asks nothing, says nothing, still looking ahead with his big, dark eyes, still as sad as ever. He accepts things as they happen.

He no longer knows tears of joy. He lives in our shadow, quiet and lonely.

The night is just like the previous ones. Without a sound, the cold continues its killer job. Huffing and puffing, the train moves in the dark. Stop and go. The thunder of the big guns and the light flashes now fill the entire sky. Have the Russians encircled us? In our corner, we squat close together and take another sugar cube.

Olomouc, Czechoslovakia. Never shall I forget that name. That is where an archangel touched me.

❖ THE DEATH ❖
OF A CHILD

On the morning of the fourth day of our deadly journey, we are thrown to the floor by the abrupt braking of the train. We hear the hissing steam escape from the locomotive. What is going on? We barely manage to get back on our feet and glimpse our surroundings. It has stopped snowing. The sun is low in the clear blue sky. The train has stopped between two small hills. On all sides we hear the frightening thunder of frontline guns. From the direction of the locomotive, the Germans are barking their orders. Our guards jump out of the car.

Within a few seconds, the train is surrounded by German troops. They are facing us from fifteen yards away, their threatening rifles at the ready. "This is the end of our journey. They are going to liquidate us," I hear somebody say. With pounding hearts, we look over the edge at the helmets and the rifles. Motionless, we stand eye to eye, the defenders and the torturers.

From behind the hills, the guns are roaring and the earth shakes. Minutes go by. Some of us sag back to the floor between the dead of the previous night. The Germans are just standing in the snow. What are they waiting for? The tension rises. We feel that the decisive moment has arrived. We are sure we are going to die. Someone starts to sob softly, from the depth of his soul. It sounds more like relief, upcoming redemption, than desperation. Resignation rather than sorrow.

Benno has now gotten right next to me in this hour of the truth. Silently, we face death. "I don't understand," I whisper without taking my eyes from the rifles. "Why is nothing happening?" No answer. Benno is puzzled, too. The horizon is afire, the sky torn apart. This picture of us and the train is bizarre. Time seems frozen. Life has no part in it.

At the end of our car, something drops in the snow. Like puppets, we all stretch our necks simultaneously. A tiny figure in a coat with too-long sleeves works his way through the snow in the direction of the helmets. Piszta! What is that child doing there? Has he lost his mind? Paralyzed, I watch the boy lift his legs with every step through the deep snow. He is about six yards away now. A hoarse shout from the direction of a car: "Hey, you!" Piszta looks up, startled, and turns slightly toward the sound. Immediately two gunshots fill the valley. The hills bounce back the sound, many times. Like thunder, it pounds our ears and pierces our brain.

Piszta. I want to call out his name, over the hills, the fields, the villages, the cities. But I can't. My voice dies down before it makes a sound. Fear suffocates me.

There he lies, thrown backward in the snow, two red stains starting to fill his torn coat. Two yards away is his cap with its familiar string. For the first time, we see his little bald head.

In our heads we still hear the sound. Without a move, we keep hanging over the side of the car and stare at the growing stain in the snow. How many dead have we seen? We are hardened. We can grab corpses and throw them off the train. By the dozen, we saw them at Buna. We walked past them, stepped over them, or hauled them back with us on the evening march to Monowitz. Their faces have disappeared with time. But this child, Piszta. His image is forever etched in my mind.

Then, as if the death of our little friend was their sign, the guards suddenly start to move. They spread out and take their places in the cars. Automatically, we duck and start to pick up and move the corpses of those who, only yesterday, had been our neighbors. With all the strength that's left in us, we drop them into the snow.

When the train starts to move again, I watch the dots alongside the road getting smaller and smaller. How many? Twenty? Thirty? A bit to the left, a separate little dot. I try to keep my eyes on that one spot for as long as possible.

As the train picks up speed, I vow that one little un-buried body will someday be mentioned in memory of all those thousands who disappeared anonymously.

Like a snake looking for a safe place in the middle of two brush-fires, the train glides through the front lines. Benno and I have quietly retreated to our corner. Piszta's death has deeply touched us, as if we suddenly have become more vulnerable, as if our defenses and will to survive have diminished. Forever, that one question keeps coming back. Why? Why did he jump off the train? We will never know.

Again the train slows. We no longer look over the sides. Waiting forever. Moving again. The sky closes, and a sudden breeze whips us with fine crystals of snow. Another evening, another night. Somebody moans for his mother. In the dark, Benno and I are recovering our "treasures." Not much is left. We keep very quiet. It could cost us our lives.

In the middle of the day, we enter a big city. "Prague," Benno, says. The train hisses its steam through a low-lying stretch of the railway far below the streets. On an overpass, people have gathered. Somber and curious, they look down at the moving human garbage cans. Suddenly bread and apples are raining down. Apparently they had been prepared for our arrival; we are not the first ones, obviously.

A few loaves drop into our car. Just as before, a severe struggle fol-lows. Benno and I look at each other. No, we are not risking our lives for a piece of bread. We stay on the sidelines, knowing we still have enough left for maybe one or two days.

When the fighting is over, only a few have managed to get some bread, and it has disappeared immediately into their hungry stomachs.

Exhausted, the losers remain seated on the floor. It is not clear whether they can all get back up again.

Somewhere on a deserted track of the Prague railway station we come to a standstill. The endless waiting starts all over again. At a distance, the SS are keeping the train within firing range. Only in the evening, we leave the city. More corpses at our feet. Never was there a colder night.

We are approaching the edge of madness. The sick are yelling, hallucinating feverishly. There is screaming and begging for water. Death is becoming uglier. Even the strongest are at the brink of exhaustion. Benno and I, too, feel we won't be able to hold out much longer. At wit's end-may God forgive us-we are piling the corpses on top of us to get some shelter from the cold. Buried by the dead, we wait for the end that is bound to come. I don't know if another day and night have passed after Prague.

At the end of the day, when everybody has long since reconciled himself with the inevitable, we can suddenly leave the train. We had not even noticed it had stopped! Emaciated prisoners in nondescript clothing help us off the train.

"Buchenwald," they answer our question. There are only a few of us left. Slowly we shuffle alongside the yellowish military-like buildings until we reach the old familiar barbed wire. A wrought-iron gate in the fence has the words TO EACH HIS OWN written on it.

❖ THE WATCH ❖

Over the campgrounds we are taken to a big brick building. The guards apathetically chase us through a door; they have their hands full with the crowd. Here and there, people are hit, but they don't care. Just hold on a little longer, then rest and a bed.

The familiar counting: Count and wait, count again and wait. After some time, an order: "Undress!" In a few seconds we are naked, our stinking clothes at our feet.

A little farther down, there are two SS officers. We have to walk past them, hands in the air and mouths open. "I have a little problem," Benno whispers to me. Carefully, he shows me the palms of his half-opened hands. Between my teeth, I whistle, stunned. Two watches, one round, one square! He has smuggled them with him for the entire trip. What a wheeler-dealer!

"Here, take one, put it into your anus." He pushes the square watch into my hand and immediately puts the round one into his anus. Hesitatingly, I follow his example. I manage, but the angular shape makes it painful. "Nice guy you are," I complain as we start to walk. "I can barely walk with that stupid thing back there!" Benno doesn't answer. We are close to the two SS men now.

With my buttocks squeezed together, I walk by them, in an effeminate manner. "Look," one guard says to the other, "that one walks like a scorched pig." They both burst out laughing. I hurry to get out of their sight. A bit farther along, the line comes to a halt. Everybody is being dunked into a big wood barrel with Lysol. Now what? That's going to be the end of the watches. "In your mouth," Benno points without a word and immediately gives the example. In my mouth? Is he crazy? But I have no choice. We are close already.

I take the watch out of my ass and in one move put it into my mouth. Then we plunge into the Lysol. A bit later, we dry one another with burlap sacks. Immediately after the Lysol bath I take the watch out of my mouth in total disgust. Four, five times, I spit out my saliva.

Still nude, we arrive at a wide concrete staircase that leads downward. "Go down, hurry." We stumble down into a narrow corridor. It is pitch dark and freezing cold. We shiver as we walk one behind the other in this subterranean tunnel. With every step, our fear increases. What are they going to do with us? We are naked, and it is dark. Is this the place of execution? We are completely trapped in here.

Then, all of a sudden, we trip over steps that lead back up. It gradually gets lighter. An open door and we are in a big room. Daylight and space! A sigh of relief. Through the tunnel, we have arrived in another building. "Get dressed." From a corner, a variety of clothing is thrown at us. For ten months I have worn that hated striped prison outfit. All that time I have looked forward to the day that I would be able to swap it for civilian clothes. Now that that moment is here, I'm not sure I'm all that glad.

When I'm finally fully dressed, I'm wearing beach pants with ridiculously wide legs, a much-too-short jacket, and a makeshift cap. The previous owner must have had a gigantic head.

Everybody looks ridiculous. Some are walking around like bellboys, circus directors, and cavalry soldiers from the nineteenth century. We are looking at one another, not knowing whether to laugh or cry. Then, "Off you go!"

Emaciated human beings in carnival-like costumes are start-ing to move. That's how we arrive at our new housing in the "little camp." Meanwhile, I have returned Benno's square watch. "Thanks, little Louis."

By Louis de Wijze

❖ THE WITNESS ❖

At the courtyard of the little camp, we are subdivided into groups of one hundred. Because of all the confusion, Benno ends up in a different group. At a distance, we wave at each other.

On the way to our designated barrack, we walk past the washhouse. Dozens of corpses are piled up against the walls. The view of the blue, stiff skeletons no longer affects us. How many dead have we counted among ourselves? We walk past them without a sigh, without even blinking our eyes.

At the door of our barrack, there is soup! We slowly shuffle past the kettle in two rows. Everybody gets a plate and a spoon. We greedily slurp our plate and lick it clean until it shines. It is our first warm meal in a week. Finally a bed, finally rest for our broken bodies. Nobody cares that we are sleeping in less than a pigsty. Just lying down flat, no more weight on our legs, no more walking, not one more minute standing up. We can't believe it. We don't feel how rough and hard the planks are. And who cares whether we are lying fourteen next to one another, and four stories high? Peace, finally peace.

Two days and nights go by without anything worth mentioning. All that time, we stay in our barrack. We go out only to use the bathroom. The shit is piled up many inches high. Directly across the small camp, in a different corner, is the crematorium.

As we entered Buchenwald, we had seen the chimney. But death strikes so fast here that the ovens are incapable of handling the human load. The heap of corpses near the bathroom grows every day.

We live in complete seclusion. Bored, we just hang around in the barrack, or lie on our planks. We have not heard any news for days. We vegetate in a grim underworld.

In the middle of one night, roll call. We curse. They could count us all day long, as often as they like, but what do they do? Just to irritate us, in the middle of the cold winter night they chase us out. What crazy brain devises such a thing? Shivering, we suffer the familiar ritual.

Then something happens. A Jehovah's Witness in the front row suddenly gets whacked on the shoulder with a bull's pizzle. The guard rants and raves like a rabid dog. "What are you grinning at? We will teach you a little lesson, you scurvy Witness!" And again the pizzle rains down on the man. To everyone's amazement, the man does not flinch. Defiantly, he keeps upright. "You can hit me," he says almost triumphantly. "You can only touch my body, my soul is untouchable, it belongs to God." He keeps smiling at the tormentor who hits him one more time, hesitates, and then walks away.

In admiration, we watch the man who, unobtrusively now, stands among us with a bowed head. What courage, what strength he had shown! Then the roll call is over.

Blue with cold, after an hour and a half we crawl back into our cages. In the dark on my plank I am trying to estimate the number of prisoners in the barrack. Fourteen, side by side, four stories high, times about twenty sleep units. We must be about a thousand under one roof.

By Louis de Wijze

❖ THE MARCH NORTH ❖

Early the sixth or seventh day of our stay at Buchenwald, a prisoner enters our barrack. I have not seen him before. "Is there anybody here from Nijmegen?" I hear him ask in German. Surprised, I get up. "Yes, I am," I say as I walk over to him. "What is the matter?" "Nothing. Let me take you to a friend from Nijmegen. Follow me." The stranger turns around and walks outside. I follow, quite puzzled. A friend from Nijmegen? Here, in Buchenwald? Whom could that be?

In silence, my messenger leads me. At the double barbed wire that separates the small camp from the big one, he talks with the guards. Then he beckons me to follow him again. For the first time since our arrival, I am out of the little camp. It is still bitter cold. We walk between the barracks all the way to the other side of the camp. "It is here," my companion says in front of a barrack. "He is waiting for you inside. See you later." And off he goes.

I nervously open the door and go inside. Behind a big wooden table, his eyes focused on the door, I see him. With his broad smile, he laughs at me. I would have recognized Piet de Booy anywhere; since our soccer years he has not changed a bit. He jumps up from behind the table, and his chair falls backward. "Louis, man, am I glad to see you!"

We grab each other, smile, and shake our heads in disbelief. What a miracle! Piet pulls me over to the table. Seated opposite me, he tells me how, a few days ago, he heard that some Dutchmen were on the transport from Auschwitz, and even someone from Nijmegen. Somehow he had found out that "someone" was me. Through somebody with good connections, he had managed to get me out of the little camp for a short visit. "And here we are," Piet says, still beaming.

"But what are you doing here in Buchenwald?" I ask him. Piet's face turns serious. He tells me he has been in the Resistance. When it got too dangerous, he had to disappear from view. He had tried to get to Switzerland, but close to the Swiss border he had been caught. He ended up here in Buchenwald a few months ago.

I tell him my story, and we spend the entire afternoon telling and listening. Quietly, and with a look of disbelief, Piet listens to my horror stories of Auschwitz. Time goes by unnoticed. Suddenly Piet sees that dusk has already set in, and he jumps up. "Hurry, Louis," he says, slightly panicky, "it's almost dark. Everybody has to be in shortly. In case of an air raid, all lights are switched off and the Krauts turn off the power from the fence and let their dogs roam free, so nobody can be outside. You better hurry, or you'll be late!" With a quick hug, we say good-bye.

When I step outside, the companion from before is waiting for me. Let's go, he signals. He takes me to the barbed-wire fence, chats with the guards, and leaves with a brief wave. I have barely arrived at my barrack as the sirens are starting to sound.

"Out, out, you scum, out!" Contrary to previous days, we have to get out of the barrack the next morning. It is still very early. We are shivering and yawning in the courtyard. Count, recount, wait. Then an order: "Line up in rows of five." We look at one another in surprise. Are we leaving here? A few minutes later our entire barrack marches out of the little camp. As we leave the main entrance, I realize I am leaving Benno behind. I have not seen him since our arrival in Buchenwald a week ago. I have to continue without my friend and protector. To each his own.

Ten minutes later we are standing next to a goods train. I count twenty railroad cars. In groups of fifty, we are driven into the cars.

These cars are covered, not the open type like before. The steam whistle yells, and the train starts to move.

I have managed to get a spot against the side of the car, so I have support. Fortunately, there is enough space to sit on the floor. Opposite us, as always, are a few armed SS officers. The sliding door is, for some unknown reason, left slightly ajar. On the outside, a bolt keeps it locked. The train is traveling at a high speed, without stopping anywhere. We are shivering in the cold as we pass villages and towns, ride through hills and forests, straight north, deeper into Germany.

The prisoner next to me, a German Jew, tells me with tears in his eyes how he found his brother in Buchenwald after three years. Both had previously been deported to the east and had lost sight of each other. He had been convinced his brother had died. But after the gruesome evacuation from the east, he had found, to his unimaginable joy, his presumed-dead brother. Highly emotional, with eyes beaming, he tells me, "I am so happy we both survived. I am sure everything will be over within a few weeks."

His story has touched me. Would anyone in my family still be alive?

Hours have passed as we go by Blankenberg. It has to be around noon. Then, a few miles farther, it happens. The train brakes in full force. We have barely come to a halt when the shrill sound of dive-bombers comes from above.

A bang, then the hissing of escaping steam: The locomotive's boiler has been hit! We duck as a hail of bullets rains down upon our car. Screaming and yelling, blood all around. It is a hell. Directly in front of me, I see another prisoner's head split in two by a projectile. I scream as pieces of his brain come sliding down my jacket.

I jump up and try to push my neighbor aside to reach the door, but the man who had just been telling me about his brother now sits lifeless against the wall. From a little black hole in the middle of his forehead, a trickle of blood runs down. For the second time, we hear the frightening screech of the bombers. I dive over my neighbor to a far corner. An animal-like howling fills our car when we get hit again.

"Out! We have to get out!" I hear myself scream. Already at the door, I stick my arm outside and grab the bolt, and with a simple move I release the door. I push it open and jump off. Those who escaped the bullets roll off the slope and run like crazy over a frozen, stubbled field. Here they come again! We drop on our bellies, arms over our heads, shaking like leaves, waiting for the bullets, and the end. But miraculously, right above us, the planes pull back up with an ear-shattering noise and disappear as fast as they appeared.

Did the pilots recognize that we were civilians, not soldiers? We stay down a little longer, then hurry back to the train. From the direction of the railroad, an ashen-faced SS officer walks toward me. With both hands, he is holding the organs that are spilling from his split belly. Flabbergasted, I step aside. The man continues a few more steps and collapses.

Immense chaos reigns on the train. The air is filled with moaning and groaning. There are dead and wounded everywhere, blood, blood, and more blood. All of a sudden, everything starts to spin. I squat on the ground to vomit.

"Dumdum bullets," I hear someone shout. "They've used dumdum bullets. They are split open completely!"

Shouting SS officers are running toward us. Everybody who is unhurt is chased to a spot about fifty yards from the train. From a distance, we see prisoners carry the casualties off the train.

"Look," someone next to me says. People from a nearby village are running across the field, with sheets and bandages. "Back, go back. You are not allowed to approach the train." The villagers stare at the SS in disbelief. They want to help. Why can't they go through? But the uniforms are coming closer, with a deadly threat. Stupefied, the civilians start to leave while they continue to look back to the horrible scene at the train.

Shivering from the cold, we see the dead being loaded onto the last car. It is unclear what happens to the wounded. My head is still spinning. Half dazed, I sit on the ground. How can I possibly still be alive? Almost everyone around me got killed.

More than an hour later, another locomotive arrives and pulls our train with the casualties out of there. Two hundred and twenty casualties, we've heard the SS shout. Back to the railroad, escorted by guards on both sides, we walk north. To the right, in a shallow valley amid the rolling hills, we see the village where the civilians had come from.

After about a fifteen-minute walk, we leave the railroad and turn right. We walk on the wooden sleepers; the rails have not yet been laid. The railroad-to-be leads straight to a wooded hill that looks like a giant molehill that just happens to sit there all by itself. When we get there, the wooden sleepers disappear through a high entrance in a dark tunnel.

Over a sandy path at the bottom of the hill, we turn toward the edge of the forest. A little later we arrive at a barbed-wire fence. Left and right there are wooden watch-towers with heavily armed guards. Through a simple wooden gate, we enter the campgrounds. At about fifteen yards' distance, we see the first prisoner. He is tied to a pole, hands behind his back, a heavy piece of iron hanging around his neck. One of our guards grins when he sees us looking at the poor man.

"Tried to escape," he says. Tried to escape! Welcome to Langen-stein-Zwieberge!

❖ THE MALACHITE ❖ COMMAND

As usual, we are soon standing in a meadow for a roll call, our pale, drawn faces still overwhelmed by the images of the previous hours.

Langenstein-Zwieberge is but a small camp, maybe a few dozen barracks, mostly hidden among the trees. It takes a while before the Germans are satisfied that the numbers are correctly recorded. The shooting at the train has apparently hampered a proper counting.

A German civilian positions himself in front of us. Why are these people always yelling? Why does every word sound like they're spitting a nail? He wants to know who among us is a blacksmith. Here and there a hand goes up.

"Step forward!" About ten men start to move. I hesitate for a second. Craftsmen usually get the best jobs. But a blacksmith? Why not? *Quickly*, I join them.

"Show your hands!" Slowly the German walks past the line and inspects our hands. As he arrives near me, he stops and looks angrily at me. "You, a blacksmith?" he shouts. "Out of my sight or else .. . !" He is ready to hit me, but I've already jumped back into the group. I look at my hands. They are the hands of an office clerk, smooth and unblemished.

A little later he assigns each group its barrack number. Then we can go. Still unfamiliar with the area, we start to look for our new "home."

Inside, the atmosphere is desolate. Around a little stove squat emaciated men with hollow, baggy eyes. Some of them are coughing badly. "You got any bread?" Someone extends a bony claw toward me. I push it aside and walk to the dorm. Just as in Monowitz, the bunk beds are slightly apart. I lie down on one of the lower bunks.

That night, I find out that Langenstein-Zwieberge is the outside camp unit of Buchenwald. This camp hidden in the mountains houses approximately five thousand prisoners from all over Europe: French, Belgians, Germans, Poles, Russians, Italians, Czechs, and, apparently, a few Dutch.

It is hidden for good reason. Top-secretly, in subterranean tunnels, the prisoners are building a huge factory for the production of a new secret weapon. The people in my barrack tell me there is a network of tunnels under the mountain, miles and miles long.

It's my first working day and still pitch dark as the guards start to knock their sticks on the wooden walls of the barracks. "Get up!"

It is four in the morning. We hurry to the washrooms. Just as in Buchenwald, the floors are covered in human feces. From there, we rush to get some coffee made out of acorns and use that to wash down some pieces of bread. Four-thirty sharp, we are ready for the roll call.

The long waiting has started again. It is freezing cold. Within half an hour a few prisoners have already succumbed. After we leave, they will be taken to the sick bay by the cleaning crew. At about five-thirty we start to march, unit after unit. No orchestra here to brighten up the day with march music! "Keep walking. Hurry up, lazy pigs!" With their sticks, the SS try to get us into a light jog.

Upon our arrival at the mountain, our unit is taken through a labyrinth of dark corridors to our work site. At the end of a dead-end tunnel, we stop. Work is simple but hard. With our bare hands, we have to throw hundreds of pieces of malachite, which lie spread on the ground after an explosion, into little lorries that are riding on a minirailroad through the tunnel.

Our foreman, a German civilian who looks calm and friendly, is being addressed as "Drilling Master." With a huge drill, maybe two yards long, he drills deep holes in the rocks. Then sticks of dynamite are put into the holes. Before the wiring, we walk off to a safe distance of several hundred yards. After the dust of the explosion has settled, we walk back, led by the drilling master. With a long stick, he taps the ceiling to find out if there is any danger of falling rocks.

We work without interruption for six hours. Every once in a while the guards come to check. We await them with great fear, because each time they shower us with their sticks. We have to work ever faster.

Midmoming, one of our comrades dies. He just drops dead on the spot. My boss tells me and another newcomer to take the victim to the entrance of the tunnel and leave him there. When we pick him up by his arms and legs, I am startled that he is no heavier than a child.

Exhausted, we sit down at noontime. Our backs leaning against the rocks, we eat our last bits of bread.

Before we know it, our half-hour lunch break is over. Our guards appear and drive us back to work. Five long hours to go. At the end of the day, totally broken, we walk back through the tunnels to the outside. One working day; two dead.

I should have known. Before going back to the camp, we have to be counted. Fortunately, it is over soon. It is way past six when we enter the gate, but to think that we would finally get our soup would be foolish. We are going straight to a place for a roll call. What? Another roll call? We are being humiliated once again.

After a week I am promoted to helper of the drilling master. I don't know why he picked me, but I am very happy about it. My work suddenly becomes much lighter. I help him to operate that gigantic drill, handle the dynamite and the wiring, and basically do what he tells me to do.

We get along very well. He tells me he lives in a small village close to Aachen, near the Dutch border. He is a miner by profession. In a soft tone of voice, he talks about his wife and children, whom he has not seen in a long time. He is a gentle human being, and I notice he is greatly distressed by our suffering.

During lunch break of our first working day together, we sit next to each other, slightly away from the others. He has his lunch box next to him. Time and again, my eyes are pulled in the direction of those delicious sandwiches. Suddenly, he takes a double sandwich with sausage out of the box and puts it into my hands. As I start to open my mouth to thank him, he gestures to me to be silent. Like a hungry wolf, I attack my meal, and in no time it's gone. When I look up at him, I see his moist, glistening eyes. He gets up quickly and turns around to blow his nose very hard.

That night, after we creep out of the womb of the mountain, a nasty surprise awaits us. Almost daily, we smuggle pieces of wood in the legs of our trousers from the tunnels back to the camp. It is the only way to get sufficient firewood for our stove. It is still freezing, and the evenings and nights are brutally cold because the walls of the barracks are paper thin.

Although I have occasionally taken firewood along with me, today I have been unable to get hold of any. That was lucky, because one by one we have to walk past an SS officer who taps with his stick at our legs and backs. Apparently the Krauts have been tipped off about our smuggling. One of the prisoners of our unit gets caught.

"Ah, Mr. Woodleg!" the officer shouts when his tapping reveals that the man has hidden some wood beneath his clothing. "Ah, you have got yourself a prosthesis?" In a rage, he starts to pound the victim until the man, bleeding profusely, collapses. Soon after, we take him back, hanging in between us. The SS officer has made a note of his number.

❦

❖ THE NINE ❖ HUNDRED

Day in, day out, we are working like moles under the ground. Our life is gray, with nothing to look forward to. Every day is like the previous one: wake up, roll call, eleven to twelve hours of hard labor in the mine, roll call, and a few hours' sleep.

In the camp there is absolutely nothing to do, not a single form of entertainment, no distraction, no chance to organize anything. There is no sense of solidarity, let alone friendship. After all these weeks I still feel alone here. No one to share my daily worries. It is as if the camp is covered by a veil that obscures every little bit of hope and optimism.

The food situation in Langenstein-Zwieberge is even worse than in Monowitz. Every day we receive seven ounces of bread, sometimes with a slice of margarine or a bit of marmalade. In the morning and at lunch, there is a mug of muddy coffee. We have no idea what the basis is for our nightly portion of soup, but the nutritional value is very low.

Carrying the kettle of soup is quite a venture each day. Two prisoners take the fifty-two-gallon kettle sitting on two supporting sticks from the kitchen to the barrack. They have to maneuver carefully, between the trees. Everywhere, branches and rocks protrude, making it an extremely arduous task to transport the kettle without spilling.

From behind the trees, prisoners jump out and plunge their plates in the caldron and immediately disappear. They are mainly Russians. The carriers are too busy keeping their balance to do anything about it. Watery soup and a piece of bread: totally inadequate to sustain hard labor and survive.

At the beginning of March, almost everyone has diarrhea, but there are no medicines to treat it. Every day the death toll rises. Until recently the corpses were picked up by an old farmer from Langenstein in his horse-drawn cart and taken to the crematorium about six miles away in a village called Quedlinburg. But for a while now the crematorium has been unable to handle the load. As a consequence, the corpses keep piling up at the "corpse cellar." Hundreds of them are lying against the walls outside.

Strange rumors are starting to circulate around the camp. It is said that prisoners have cut off pieces of the corpses in the corpse cellar. First we shrug at this news. But the rumors continue. When somebody tells me he himself has eaten human flesh, for me the proof is there. The Krauts now have gotten us to the point that we are able to eat one another. In our school years, we had heard of this concept of primitive societies eating humans. Now we are just like them, cannibals.

At one point during my work in the tunnels I get severe intestinal cramps. They are so bad that I immediately have to empty my bowels. I tell my boss about it, and he gives me permission to go. But where to? I search for a private spot, but it is very crowded in the tunnel, like a busy street. Nowhere to drop my pants. Or is there?

As unobtrusively as possible, I walk to the lorries; maybe I can use one of them. I quickly climb into the closest one and squat down. Just in time. What a relief! But in the middle of it all, the little locomotive starts its engine and haltingly begins to move. I freeze. Like lightning, I pull up my pants, but it is too late. The speed is too great to jump out. It would be suicide.

I cautiously stick my head over the edge of the lorry. For several minutes, we rush through the maze, in and out of tunnels. Then the train brakes. I dive back down. There are voices all around me. I hear footsteps. I wait for the sounds to disappear. Then I come out of my hiding place and jump off the little car.

I am in a gigantic subterranean hall, at the end of which I see the blue sky. The walls of the hall are tiled, like a slaughterhouse. Rails and lorries are everywhere. Prisoners and guards are walking back and forth.

I walk toward the daylight. I recognize the place: It has to be the entrance to the mountain. Through that big opening, we had seen the little railroad lead into the mountain. I stop about twenty yards from the entrance. In the blue sky, I see a plane with another little plane on top of it. Incredulously, I look at this curious double plane. I have never seen anything like it! Could this be one of their secret weapons?

"What are you doing here?" A guard with a threatening voice comes up to me. Before I can answer, he has hit me in the neck, right where I have a big ulcer that has been bothering me. I cringe and rush back in the direction of the tunnel. Fortunately, the guard does not pursue me. I walk into a sparsely lit corridor and stop at an intersection. Now what?

For ages I wander through dark tunnels until, finally, I arrive at a familiar looking area. Back at my work site, I tell my drilling master exactly what happened. Luckily, he laughs about it. "Let's go back to work, lunch break has long since passed." I am surprised. Have I been gone that long?

When we return to start our drilling and I hastily put some bread-crumbs in my mouth, my boss puts his hand in the pocket of his coverall. He has saved me another double sandwich!

A few days later at the morning roll call, they ask for volunteers to fetch bread. We know that the term "fetch bread" often is a ruse that can mean any nasty task. But the temptation is too great and I volunteer. You never know. Soon it turns out we have been fooled again.

After the others have gone to the mine, we are told we have to dig a mass grave near the cellar where the corpses are. About sixty prisoners are directed to the spot. Six others, including myself, are taken out of the camp to a plateau that borders a hill maybe a hundred and fifty yards from the fence. We find a long, deep trench that, apparently, has been dug before by other prisoners. It is about ten yards long, two yards wide, and three yards deep. Four prisoners have to go into the trench; another one and I stay on top at the edge.

After a while, we see six prisoners carrying a box up the hill from the camp, one box every one or two minutes. Each one contains two corpses. After they put down the box, we lift the corpses out and slide them down a plank into the grave. Down in the grave, they are laid side by side, width-wise. The stench is unbearable. Sometimes the corpses have degenerated to the point that we can feel only rough skin with bones sort of hanging loosely inside.

It is like a bad dream. Box after box, body after body. Grab, lift, roll, grab, lift, roll . . . I'm trying not to think. Don't look, don't feel. They keep coming, hour after hour. Every time a layer has been put over the entire length, the four trench men climb out and, together, we spread quicklime in the pit. Then we start with the next layer. Finally, as the dusk sets in, we are finished. The trench is full. Nine hundred corpses went through our hands. Like broken men, we stumble back to the camp.

In ice-cold water from the tap, I wash myself-twice-from head to toe, but I cannot wash away the images in my head.

❖ Freedom Nears ❖

At the end of March, I suffer a bout of phlegmon again! This time my right hand is infected. In just one day it swells to the size of a bear's paw. The pain is so severe I can't hold out. The drilling master urges me to have it treated at the sick bay immediately. After the soup, I go there.

The crowd is incredible. Dozens of patients are ahead of me. Just as in Monowitz, some of them have death in their eyes. Unstable, they stand in line, just skin and bones, hollow-eyed. After an hour and a half, it is my turn.

A young nurse inspects my swollen hand. "Sorry, but I'm going to have to cut this," he says. "You better grit your teeth." I swallow nervously. He takes a small, sharp knife and holds it momentarily in a flame. He lets it cool, then grabs my wrist and pins it under his hand on the table. "Here we go!" he says, and I feel a terrible pain go through my hand. It repeats itself twice. I scream. Then it's over.

With a paper towel, the nurse catches the liquid and blood that ooze from the three incisions. "That's that," he says, "not too bad." I am silent. Pale as a ghost, I sit down on a little three-legged stool. Not too bad? What is he talking about? Then he wraps my hand in a paper bandage and tells me to come back in two days. Meanwhile, I cannot work. "Next. . ."

Two days off. I am not happy. I am missing my extra sandwiches. I just hang around the camp. The first spring rain has changed the campsite into a desolate pool of mud. It really depresses me. At the corpse cellar, another hundred bodies have piled up. The stench is putrid.

The first evening of my sick leave, the soup is delivered to our barrack. The units have not returned from the tunnels. The soup is made of wild chestnuts. I hesitate, but the temptation is too great. With my plate, I rush to the kettle. Like a pig, I gobble up two full plates. Just as I am about to start my third plate, the door flies open.

"Damn it, that pig is eating all our soup!" Ranting and raving, my comrades storm at me. I'm being pushed and shoved. Their clenched fists are right in front of my eyes. Somebody spits in my face. Full of shame, I stay back.

At the beginning of April, we hear that the Allies are making a lot of headway. Supposedly the Americans are only twenty-five miles away. Indeed, we have heard the frontline noise getting louder and louder. Now and then, fighter planes fly over the hills. My hand has healed almost completely, without any medication.

A few days later the camp commander himself shows up at the evening roll call. It is the first time I've seen him. He makes a confused speech that basically comes down to our no longer having to work-do we hear this right?-because of the general state of exhaustion.

That night the entire camp is in disarray. Everybody speculates about the Germans' sudden change of heart. Plenty of rumors are circulating. Somebody "knows" that large amounts of explosives have been placed in special tunnels and there is a plan to liquidate the entire camp population. Others think that we will be abandoned, left to our own devices, because the Germans are about to leave.

The next day, dozens of bombers fill the sky. Within minutes, everything behind the hills is on fire. Our barracks are shaken by the explosions. Black smoke plumes rise to the sky. Undoubtedly, Halberstadt has been bombed. The town, about four miles from Langenstein, is in flames.

During the course of he day, the Germans rush to pack their bags, and it looks like they are about to bolt. But our fear grows. Is it really happening? Are we going to be free within a few days?

At night, the SS calls in the leaders of the barracks. When they return, they are waving their caps. "We can wait for the Americans," they call from the distance. "The Germans are leaving. We are on our own!" We grab one another and start to laugh. "We made it! We are free!"

That very same night, a meeting takes place in one of our barracks. A lot has to be organized for the coming days: the transport of food to the camp, burial of the dead, medicines for the sick, that's urgent. Very late, I get back on my straw bed, but I don't get much sleep.

❖ The Death March ❖

If you had been French ...

We are mad, disappointed but mainly very upset, when the next morning we hear that the camp will be evacuated after all. All our plans and ideas of yesterday immediately lose their validity.

That entire morning the chaos in the camp is enormous. Hours go by, and there is no indication whatsoever if or when we'll leave. There is a growing hope the Americans will liberate us before the evacuation. They have got to be close, because the air is filled with the sound of roaring guns. The fighter planes are flying low over the woods around us. Is it going to happen?

Late in the afternoon they order us to assemble for roll call. Every able body will come along. Only the very ill can stay in the barracks. Everyone who can possibly walk assembles; nobody wants to stay behind. We are convinced that those who stay behind will be liquidated. One last roll call. Some, who are too weak to stand up, hold on to others. The temperature is a only bit above freezing.

I have put my khaki-colored work coveralls under my camp clothes, so I am reasonably armed against the cold. This morning, when I had my bandage changed by the nurse for the last time, I managed, when he was not looking, to snatch bandages, tape, and some kind of antiseptic. One never knows, I thought, and stashed everything carefully under my clothes.

Counting. Never was it more chaotic than now. We have to form groups of five hundred. As the counting is in full swing, we notice a horse-drawn cart just outside the camp on the sandy road. It is loaded with bread and a barrel containing some unknown liquid. So there is food and drink for the journey.

An older SS officer climbs on the cart, and the horse starts to pull. Then, group after group, we march out of the camp toward Quedlinburg, a few minutes between each group. At the last watchtower, I briefly look left. A little higher up, against the hill, is the place where we buried nine hundred bodies in a mass grave.

Again I visualize the tangled corpses covered with quicklime. The grave must be closed by now. Will anybody ever find that spot again?

We move slowly through the hilly country. After only a few hundred yards, the trip is tough already because the road climbs almost unnoticeably. In less than a mile, the first victim is a fact. A little bit in front of me, someone has collapsed. Two guards drag him to a trench. A shot echoes between the hills.

"Continue. Keep walking!" And we're off again, step by step, looking down. Hours on end, over dirt roads and paved roads. Dead tired, we stumble into the falling night. One prisoner after the other cannot keep up with the pace and drops to the back of the line, to the absolute border between life and death. He who cannot keep up back there is doomed and is ruthlessly shot by SS commandos who are walking about ten yards behind the group.

In the distance, the guns are thundering relentlessly. We can hear them from three sides now. Our ghostlike faces are lit by the fires that tear open the skies. On we go. Walk, walk, walk. Will it never end? We have long since passed Quedlinburg when we are chased into a barn on the edge of a little village. Finally, a break. En masse, we enter the wide doors and fight for a spot on the concrete floor. In the corner of the barn, I see a tall wood chest. I climb on top of it, wipe off the mess, and lie down. Below, everybody is still struggling for space. Nobody sees me.

"Out! Everybody out!" It has gotten light as the SS rushes in and starts to hit the prisoners. I must have been in a deep sleep for a few hours. "Out, quickly!"

A tumultuous noise fills the barn as everybody rushes to get up. I keep still as a mouse. My brain is working full speed. Nobody can see me here. Can I take the chance? The Americans have to be close. It is a unique opportunity. The noise in the barn starts to diminish, but for some squeaking SS boots. Have they gone?

"Look on top of that chest," somebody shouts. I freeze and pretend to sleep, the only thing I can think of. A stumbling noise, the chest starts to shake. Through my barely open eyes, I see a hat and then a head appear. "Damn it! There is one here still asleep!"

I produce a long yawn as if I've just woken up from a deep sleep, pretend to be completely startled, and dash off the chest. Down there, another SS officer grabs my coat, kicks me hard in the shins a few times, and ranting and raving and hitting, chases me outside. Stumbling over my own feet, I reach the waiting group and immediately hide in it. Still panting, I wipe the sweat from my brow. That was close!

Minutes later we walk in the pale morning light out of the village. The front line is getting closer. The sounds are frightening. Mile after mile, we drag on. More and more comrades stay behind. The shots from the back tell us our ranks are getting thinner.

After a few hours we can rest on the road so that our guards can keep an eye on us. Greedily, we take a lump of bread. Then, "Let's go, move it, move it!"

We continue, hour after hour. It is getting dark again as close to a little village we recognize a few of the other groups. Our guards have their hands full herding the masses onto a sport field. In this chaos, I manage to get into the direction of the surrounding bushes. I take a quick look around. Now or never! And off I go. Through the bushes, I reach the road that leads to the village.

I have to find shelter soon; there is no strength left in me. At a short distance from the road, I see the silhouette of a farmhouse and carefully approach it. A little strip of light emanates from under the back door. With my ear on the door, I listen for a few seconds. I hear the voices of grown-ups and children. I hesitate for a moment, then I knock on the door and walk inside.

Around the kitchen table, a farmer, his wife, and three children are gathered. Bewildered eyes look at me. The father stands up.

"Could I please sleep in your barn tonight and wait for the Americans?" I promptly ask. In silence, the five keep staring at me. "Please help me! I am an escaped concentration camp prisoner," I add. The farmer's wife is now standing beside him. Momentarily, they look at each other, then the man starts to speak. "Go away. There is nothing we can do for you. You must understand that I cannot jeopardize my family. Please go! I'm sorry!" I look at the children at the table. They are still very young. They are almost hidden under the table, their scared eyes visible just above the surface. I turn around and walk out.

Outside in the dark, I get scared. My legs feel like rubber. I am so tired I can hardly walk. I have to get some rest. But what chance do I stand if I keep wandering around? Nobody is going to help an escaped prisoner in these life-threatening circumstances. It is not unthinkable that they might even surrender me. It may sound strange, but maybe the safest place to be is among my own group of prisoners.

I crawl back to the sports field. I wait in the bushes for the right moment and slip back onto the field. Back there, I cuddle up under somebody's blanket. Nobody minds another body because the closer you lie to the next person, the warmer you are and the better you are able to keep your body temperature. Soon there are three of us under one blanket, curled up like spoons, shivering and waiting for the morning.

We can't sleep because the thundering sounds of war are all around us. Grenades zoom through the air and explode ever closer to us. "Get up! Hurry! Move it!"

In the light of dawn, stiff and chilled to the bone, we barely manage to get up. Again we get a lump of bread. Shouts and orders, total pandemonium. Again I am overcome by this uncontrollable urge to flee. Again I quickly move to the shrubs and duck. "Stop! Stop right there!" A bundle of light comes my way. I lower my pants and squat down. "Did you want to escape or what?" he says and takes out his pistol. "Not at all," I say convincingly. "I had to relieve myself real badly. Diarrhea!" I stand and pull up my pants.

"What nationality?" the voice snaps. "Dutchman, from Nijmegen." "You are lucky," the voice says. "If you had been French, I would have shot you right here! Now get your butt in gear. Quick!"

A moment later, we are back with the group, and he takes me to the SS commandos who already have positioned themselves in the back. "This shitty Dutchman was trying to escape," my guard says. "Let him walk just in front of you. If he makes even one move you don't like, you shoot him!" It is now daylight, and we are ordered to leave. With guns in my back, I walk off the field.

As the skies are torn apart by heavy explosions, and planes buzz over our heads, and grenades fall all around the hamlet, we keep walking the little country road. Away from hell.

❖ THE ESCAPE ❖

With throbbing temples, we rush through a world of fire and thunder. The SS is herding us like cattle. "Move it, move it!" Gasping for air, I try to stay ahead of the guns and rifles. Right behind me, the executions continue without a pause.

A thunderous noise pounds our eardrums, and we are thrown to the ground. One, two seconds of silence, then an icy shriek. Dazed, I get up. What happened? Less than a hundred yards ahead of me, I see a big crater in the road. An entire clump of people has completely disappeared. Blood everywhere. Bodies ripped apart. The wounded are screaming and crawling to the side of the road.

Driven by pure powerlessness, we scream along. In total confusion, everybody walks back and forth. But there is the SS already. With the butts of their rifles, they start to hit us. We have to keep walking. No time for the wounded. Away from this disaster area.

They drive us quickly past the bloodbath. I am trying not to look. I have to go ahead. A bit farther down the road, our guards regain control over the group. "Go on, go on!" The consternation and the dispersion have allowed me to move up from the back. Nobody pays any attention. We hurry forward totally numbed.

Each time the fighter planes approach us, we drop on the road. On and on. After miles and miles, when we are no longer in danger of being attacked by the planes, we are allowed to sit down on the side of the road. Complete exhaustion has overtaken us, but after an hour, "Hurry, get up, we're going."

We drag our tired bodies and force our legs to walk again. For hours we continue. Another night. In the middle of the road, we huddle together in the dark, shuddering with fear. Before dawn, we leave. Behind us is only death. Not fifteen minutes pass without executions. Sometimes we pass through villages with friendly-sounding names ending with *leben* (to live): Aschersleben, Sandersleben, Alsleben.

Late in the afternoon we get bread and, suddenly, coffee. While everybody is sitting down, I crawl to the food car parked nearby. The horse stands quietly between the poles, and the old guard sits, all tucked in, on the riding box. Is he asleep? What could be in the big barrel? Very carefully, I climb on the back of the wagon and pry open the lid. Glucose! The barrel is completely full of sweet and sticky grape sugar. I grab my spoon. A spoonful of this power food immediately disappears in my mouth.

"You like it?" I almost faint! The old man has turned a little bit and grins at me. I freeze with my spoon about to go back into the barrel. Then the man turns back, pulls up the collar of his coat, and returns to his tucked-in pose. Like lightning, I plunge the spoon back into the syrup, lick it off, and slide off the car. The German has not moved. Still reeling, I join a group of prisoners far away and await the inevitable order to get moving again.

How many days and nights have we spent on the streets? Four? Five? Nobody knows. We are barely aware of being alive.

In the middle of one of those nights, we witness a gigantic distant display of fireworks. In awe, we see the dark sky change into a tapestry of exploding fireballs. Are we watching the demise of Leipzig or Dresden? We don't know.

It is morning. We get back up and start another long torture. I, too, have not much strength left in me, and won't be able to hold out much longer. In the morning light, I look at the slow-shuffling crowd around me. Once there were five hundred. Two hundred at most are left. For how long? One day? Maybe two?

Early that morning, April 15, I decide to take the first opportunity to make the ultimate escape attempt. All or nothing. I'm going to risk it.

At about ten, we stop on the fringes of a forest. We shiver as we crawl under a blanket, close together. Suddenly there is chaos. Everybody jumps up and runs in the direction of the trees where the Germans have dropped entire loaves of bread. The crowd gets involved in a tremendous brawl. I watch them intently. It gets so bad that the loaves are ripped into pieces and all that's left are crumbs.

The SS, initially just watching, now rush to the fighting crowd and with their sticks try to restore order. Now! This is the moment! Through the tall grass, I slip away, crawling like a cat. About two hundred yards away is a little bush. If I can reach that, I am safe. My head is throbbing, my breathing sounds like wheezing. Fifty yards to go. Still no shots. Next to me there is a rustling sound. Scared to death, I turn my head. Simultaneously, we look at each other: two prisoners with the same idea, at the same time. Together, we keep running.

There are the trees. We continue briefly, then we drop, exhausted. For several minutes we lie there, panting, our senses tense like a predator's. Having caught our breath, we sit up. Nothing to see, nothing to hear.

Slightly embarrassed, we look at each other and smile. The other man is in his thirties and, like me, not very tall. "What's your name?" he asks. "Louis de Wijze. I am Dutch. And you?" "Herbert Gorski, from Berlin." For a short while, we look around not knowing what to do.

"Shall we continue or wait? I am exhausted," Herbert says. "I am totally spent." "Then let's sleep a few hours first," I suggest. We settle down on a patch of soft moss where a few rays of sunlight shine through the trees. In silence, we lie on our backs. "Damn it, Herbert, we have done it!" I hear the quivering of my own voice. Herbert says nothing. I turn toward him. He is shivering. A few tears glisten on his dirty face.

Late in the afternoon, we wake up. We must have slept for hours. First we take off our striped clothes. Herbert, like me, has his civilian-looking work clothes on underneath. "It seems best to walk in the direction of the front," he suggests after we have hidden our clothing in the bushes. "We have got to reach the Americans." "All right, but we have to stay clear of villages and towns," I say.

Before we leave, I take out the bandage that I had stolen in Langenstein-Zwieberge and, with Herbert's help, wrap it around my head so that it looks like a turban. With some tape, after spilling some iodine on it, it looks like the real thing. "Well," I say, "it'll be hard for them to tell that I am an escapee from a concentration camp."

After a fifteen-minute walk, we are out of the forest. Nearby, we see a little wooden shed next to a deserted antiaircraft gun. Not a sign of life anywhere. We approach the shed and look through the little windows. Not a soul. We easily break open the locked door and are inside.

Apparently everything has been abandoned in a great hurry. Cups half full of cold coffee are on the table, and we can still smell the cigarette smoke. "Come and look here!" Herbert calls from a corner that has functioned as some sort of kitchen. Triumphantly, he shows me a huge sausage! I dash over. From the same pantry we dig up some real butter and half a loaf of bread.

We put a thick layer of butter on our bread and fill the mugs with fresh water from the tap. What a meal!

We have almost finished when the door of the shed flies open. Two German soldiers stand in the doorway. My heart beats rapidly, so terrified am I. "What is going on here?" one of them asks in a threatening manner. "We are two Dutch students," I reply quickly. "We have worked in a factory in Halberstadt but had to escape when the town was shelled. We have not eaten in days."

The soldiers look at each other. Apparently my speech has surprised them. Then the older one takes the initiative. "Yes, that is a nice story," he mocks. "Come with us." With his rifle, he gestures to us to go outside. A little later, we are walking in the direction of a spire, with rifles at our backs.

GRÄFENHAINICHEN, the sign reads as we pass the first houses. In less than ten minutes, we are locked up in the tower of the fire brigade. The door is thick and well bolted on the outside. There are no windows. Disheartened, we enter the dark. If only we could lie down, but the concrete floor is as cold as ice, so we must squat in the corner, huddled together.

"Wait, I have an idea," Herbert says. "Let's put the fire hoses on the floor!" Even if we can't sleep, at least we can rest a bit.

Before sunrise we awake to the sound of voices, as the door opens and four new prisoners are thrown inside. They are Russian POWs and, like us, are from Zwieberge. They had also escaped, only to be picked up by an army patrol. They tell us they were brutally beaten upon their arrest and are scared to death.

At daylight, the door opens. In the sharp light we see six heavily armed soldiers. Two of them come inside and tie the Russians' hands behind their backs. "Out!" Ruthlessly, they are pushed out. It is silent for a moment, then an order, followed by a barrage of gunshots.

Herbert and I look at each other. They have been executed! What about us? Is it our turn now? Seconds go by. Our hearts stop as the door opens again. A hand beckons us to step outside. Blinking our eyes against the harsh light, we stumble onto the street, stiff with fear. A little farther ahead, near a wall, the bodies of the Russians are being thrown onto a flatbed truck.

"Come along!" Almost numb, we march through the village, surrounded by soldiers. Fifteen minutes later, we are in a police cell, with two beds, a wooden table, two chairs, and a toilet. A guard silently hands us a few buttered sandwiches and a cup of coffee through a little window in the door. The fact that they feed us and the cell is relatively comfortable puts us at ease.

"I think they really believe we are laborers," Herbert says. "Otherwise they would have shot us like those Russians." We rest the whole day, napping off and on.

The sound of the thundering guns is getting closer and closer. Cars race through the village over the cobblestones, and everywhere there is yelling and screaming. Around five in the afternoon, the silent guard brings us soup. Another evening and night go by.

About seven in the morning, the little window opens up again. Bread and coffee. "Get ready for departure," the guard says before closing the window. We rush to eat our breakfast. Departure? Are we released, perhaps? Our hopes fade quickly, though, when we are led to an army truck and locked in the back.

We drive for half an hour and stop in the center of a village in front of a school building. Our guards deliver us to other soldiers and speed off again. "This is the local police station," Herbert whispers as we are taken inside. "You can tell by the silver badges on their uniforms."

They take us to a smoky and sweaty-smelling classroom. About ten other prisoners are assembled inside. "What is the name of this place?" I ask someone next to me who speaks German to his neighbor. "Eutzsch. We are close to Wittenberg on the Elbe, you know, Martin Luther's town," the answer goes.

Not long thereafter, Herbert and I are interrogated, one by one. We stick to the same story. We are students who had to work in Halberstadt. The reaction from my interviewer tells me he does not quite know how to deal with my story. As he ponders, I get a bold idea. "If you wish, I can be a messenger. I can ride a motorbike, and I speak German," I say. My plan is too transparent, and the man ignores my suggestion. He instructs someone to take me back to the classroom. Hours pass by.

Through an open door to an adjacent room, we see some POWs in strange uniforms. "You think those people are Americans?" Herbert asks. "I don't know," I answer, "but I'll soon find out." In the corner of the room, I see a broom. I grab it and enter the next room while sweeping. Nobody pays any attention as I sweep up the cigarette butts and other dirt between the soldiers. I hear a POW speak American English. So they are Americans!

"I was a prisoner from a concentration camp," I whisper in English to an elderly American soldier as I keep a keen eye on my surroundings. "What is the situation on the front?" He looks up in surprise, and a smile appears on his face. "Don't worry," he whispers back. "It won't be long. It's only a matter of days."

I nod, indicating I've understood. Unnoticed, I sweep my way back to the other room. Herbert is waiting at the door. "They are Americans. They say it won't take much longer, a few days maximum!"

That very same day, they take us and six other prisoners in an army truck to the Gestapo in Wittenberg. The eight of us are placed in one cell. Another interrogation follows. In a somber room with half-closed curtains, a pale, scrubby little civilian sits opposite me. "Student from Nijmegen?" he echoes in a hollow voice after he has listened to my story. "You must have been one of the students involved in the assassination of Police Commissioner van Dijk?" I look at him in amazement. Van Dijk has been killed by students? I can hardly suppress my feelings of joy.

For a moment I can see us again, sitting in the waiting room of the police station, as van Dijk takes our dog by the lead. He got what he deserved, my mind goes.

I tell him, truthfully, that I don't know anything about van Dijk's death. Has he really been killed by students? Those cowards! The man looks at me, puzzled. He can't quite fathom me. Nervously, he shuffles back and forth. Does he believe my story? I never find out, because after a few more stupid questions, I'm taken back to my cell. Herbert has had a similar conversation and returns in a fairly optimistic mood. "There is nothing they can do," he says. "We have no papers, and they can't check anything in Halberstadt since the Americans are probably there already. I think they will let us go free."

However, it turns out differently. That evening we are taken out of our cell and, accompanied by three guards, we march through the town to a wooden building. It turns out to be the police prison of Wittenberg. This time we are locked up separately in small cells. At least the beds have straw mattresses. Exhausted from all the tension, I lie down, but my cell turns out to be infested with lice! They jump at me by the dozen and are causing a terrible itch. All night I scratch. I don't sleep at all.

The next morning after breakfast, all prisoners are walked out of the town. At the outskirts, next to a farmhouse, we have to dig trenches. Many civilians have been summoned to help. Our guards are old soldiers who watch us from a distance but don't seem to be taking this seriously. Of course, under such circumstances, work progresses very slowly, more so because the thunder of the guns is coming closer and closer, and both workers and guards are becoming increasingly concerned. With worried looks, we regularly scout the horizon. How far would the front be now?

During our lunch break, a young man approaches our group. "Any Dutchmen here?" he asks in Dutch. "Yes, me!" I walk over to him and introduce myself. He is from a place called Hoorn on an island off the northern coast. A very nice man. He shakes my hand and Herbert's. He tells me he is doing forced labor at the adjacent farm. "Come along," he says. "The people are very friendly and won't have anything to do with the Nazis."

We slip unnoticed into the farmhouse door, and soon we're at the table eating a delectable pea soup. The farmer's wife keeps filling our plates again and again. It is delicious! Just before the work at the trench is done for the day, Herbert and I return to the group. The farmer's wife has given each of us a fitting jacket.

Back in my cell, I pay the price for the many plates of pea soup! I spend half the night on the toilet with severe intestinal cramps. The rest of the time, I fight the attacking lice again.

About six in the morning, sirens start to howl all over town. It sounds frightening. Suddenly the cell door is opened, and a guard and a commander appear. "You can go," the commander says. "The Russian tanks are close, and the town is being evacuated." A minute later Herbert and I are outside. Hundreds of frightened people throng in the direction of the Elbe.

In the midst of overloaded bicycles, handcarts, and wheelbarrows, we follow the crowd. "Wait a minute," I say to Herbert as we approach the bridge. "Let's be sensible. We need papers, official papers, to confirm we have been released and no further charges are pending against us. Otherwise, we risk being arrested again."

"Are you crazy?" Herbert asks. "We have to get out of here, now, before they besiege the town!" But I insist and keep talking until he reluctantly gives in. Against the direction of the stream of refugees, we struggle back into town. Within fifteen minutes, we arrive at the Gestapo building and ring the bell. It is the interviewer of two days ago who opens the little window in the door.

I tell him we have been released this morning and we would like a written statement confirming there are no charges against us. "Just a moment," he says and shuts the window. A short while later the door opens, and two armed policemen grab us and throw us straight back into a cell.

Herbert is furious. He rants and raves for half an hour. "I could kill you," he shouts. "What a stupid ass you are!" He stomps back and forth in the cell. "A written statement!" he scoffs. I listen to his tirade. I have indeed been incredibly stupid. It is my fault that we are in deep trouble now.

Just as Herbert has started to calm down, the mortar attack on the town begins. We put our hands over our ears to protect our eardrums, and we duck, scared to death. The walls are shaking, particles of dust are stinging our eyes. "Out! Get the hell out of here!" A guard has opened the door and is gone before we leave our cell. Bent down, we run from one building to the next, through the burning town until we manage to reach the bridge over the Elbe.

By Louis de Wijze

❖ BETWEEN THE RIVERS ❖ ELBE AND MULDE

We run up the sloping bridge and pass a woman with three daughters pushing a heavily loaded handcart. She looks pale and shocked. Herbert and I look at each other and come to her rescue. In a flash we have seen a big basket filled with bread among the furniture, suitcases, and boxes.

"Can we help you?" Herbert shouts over the thundering guns. Not waiting for an answer, we grab the cart and push it quickly over the bridge. As if chased by the devil himself, we rush on and on, pulling the rattling cart with us. We neither give ourselves nor the woman and her daughters a moment's rest. After about half an hour, when we are out of immediate danger, we slow down.

The woman walks next to us now and starts to thank us. How nice to find such helpful people in these abominable circumstances! We nod in a friendly manner, but we do not say much. It is better to see what will happen. When we take a break, we receive some bread and cold coffee.

The woman tells us she fled Berlin a day earlier and is now on her way to a castle in Bad Schmiedeberg. Her husband is a top-ranked officer in the SS and has stayed in Berlin. At the castle, more women and children of SS officers have taken refuge. She hopes to be safe there until such time as the German Army has regrouped to deal the final blow to the Allies.

Stupefied, we listen to her story. Is she really that naive to still believe in a German victory? "Shall we accompany you?" I suggest. "We are Dutch students who have worked in Halberstadt. We had to flee when the Americans started to shell the town. We will go with you to the castle. It is not a bad idea to have some protection on the way." She gratefully accepts.

We continue our trip to the south, and in the course of the afternoon we reach our destination: a big, somber castle, surrounded by some outbuildings and a farmhouse. There is furniture, cars, suitcases, and boxes all over the place. Herbert and I go to the kitchen and appoint ourselves chefs.

With the help of a few older women, we get to work. Within an hour and a half, we have prepared a meal for everyone. The storage rooms are well stocked! Being the only men around, we immediately start organizing things. We order some woman to set up the dining room and have the three daughters of our travel companion serve the meal.

Everybody accepts our authority, and by nighttime everything is reasonably organized. All families have found a spot of their own in the castle. Oddly enough, we feel relatively safe here. Nobody suspects we are escaped camp prisoners. Herbert is wearing a big cap that carefully hides his shaven head, and I am still wearing my white turban with a cap on top of it.

That night, Herbert and I get into a king-size bed in one of the outbuildings. We lie silently next to each other. It is our first night of freedom, but it is an absurd freedom. All around us, towns and villages are burning. A few hours ago, we had dinner with women and children of high-ranking SS officers. Uneasy, we toss and turn in a soft, downy bed that registers every move we make.

At breakfast we hear that our companion and her daughters, for safety reasons, have decided to travel on to family in Bad Schmiedeberg.

The incessantly roaring guns at night have scared them so much they do not want to stay a day longer. Could we maybe accompany them to Uncle Johann in Bad Schmiedeberg? It does not take us long to decide. The prospect of staying around these still-fanatical Nazi women had already prompted us to the decision to leave at our earliest convenience.

We will take the woman and her daughters to Uncle Johann, and we'll take it from there. With a fully loaded pushcart, we leave the castle. It is ten in the morning. Before noon, we arrive in Bad Schmiedeberg. Uncle Johann turns out to be a heavyset older man who happens to be in charge of the local people's movement. He is a nervous wreck because of the rapid Russian advance. However, that does not prevent him from greeting his relatives with a thunderous speech that is laced with "we will never surrender."

He raises his eyebrows as he listens to our Halberstadt story, but at the insistence of the three girls and their mother we can stay and spend the night in the hayloft in the barn.

The next morning we have a simple breakfast. Uncle Johann has already left for "work," and we take advantage of this to shamelessly enter the living room and listen to the radio for the latest war news. Within fifteen minutes, Uncle Johann suddenly appears and furiously kicks us out. We try to soothe him by pointing out that we were just trying to listen to the German broadcast, but within seconds we are back in the hayloft. We can hear the front line getting closer and closer. The sound of mortar fire and the Russian rocket launchers is frightening.

We decide to stay put and await the events. One of the girls brings us some coffee and bread around noon. We keep listening to the rumbling guns. Late in the afternoon the mother comes in. She tells us she has heard that about four miles farther down the road a train has come to a standstill. Apparently it is chock-full of food. Would we, perhaps, be willing . . . ? Of course we would! Everything that has anything to do with food always has our immediate attention.

On a lady's bicycle and with a pushcart, we follow the directions given to us. We have also taken two burlap sacks. After an hour, we arrive at the railroad and see the train sitting near a tiny station surrounded by some smaller sheds. People are walking off and on, and we see wheelbarrows, carts, and horses. Closer by, we can hardly believe our eyes. Is it a dream? In one of the railcars, people are standing waist deep in sugar. With spades, they are filling their wheelbarrows and sacks. A second car is full of jars of jam. Another one is loaded with sacks of coffee, boxes of chocolate, cigarettes, cheese, tins of ham.

We too dash to the train and start to grab everything in sight. One of us carries the goodies; the other guards the bike and pushcart and stacks everything so that it does not fall off.

It has already gotten dark when we head back. It is by no means easy to keep the bike balanced. Between the seat and the handlebars we have put a burlap sack filled with food. "That one is ours," we said as we filled it. The pushcart, too, is fully loaded with all kinds of food. Herbert, who handles the latter, has an easier job than I do with the bike.

We are walking a little country road when, close by, the roaring Russian guns start to fire in the direction of Bad Schmiedeberg. The grenades and rockets zoom just over our heads. We let go of the bike and the cart and throw ourselves to the ground. That very same moment, I feel a stinging pain in my lower leg.

"I am hit," I shout at Herbert, who lies next to me. I point to my shoe that is starting to ooze blood. He quickly crawls over to me, rolls up my pant leg, and examines my foot. "Nothing serious," he yells, "just a deep cut." With his handkerchief, he applies an emergency dressing over the wound in order to stop the bleeding.

Some time later, when the shelling has moved elsewhere, we dare get up. Herbert helps me back onto the bike. I use my good leg to keep the balance, and Herbert pushes my bike from the rear with one hand while pulling his cart with the other. In the pitch-dark night, we arrive at Bad Schmiedeberg.

The next morning, after a relatively quiet night, suddenly everything is on high alert. The sound of sirens, cars racing through the streets, and hundreds of people trekking southwest is whirling around us. When we enter the kitchen, we hear that Uncle "We Never Surrender" fled hours ago in total panic. The mother and her three daughters are about to leave. They have already loaded their possessions onto the handcart. Herbert and I quickly grab our food sacks (we had split everything last night), load them on the bike, and together with the women, we join the stream of refugees.

The sky is filled with black smoke. The guns never seem to stop. In the midst of this mass evacuation of frightened women, children, and the elderly, we drag our bike over the congested roads in the direction of Bad Düben. Within fifteen minutes we are told we can't go any farther. There is heavy fighting a little way down the road.

We leave the road and walk into the woods in small groups. My foot is starting to sting more and more. Last night we applied a bandage to it as best we could, but the wound is so serious that with each step it feels like somebody is stabbing me. I stumble and limp to keep up with the pace of the group. I am sweating profusely.

Now and then, SS patrols searching for deserters come our way. Fortunately, they are not interested in Herbert and me; we probably don't look like we ever belonged to this German terror organization. Still, we are a little worried. Hidden between the women and children, we continue.

Just ahead of us, we hear some yelling. The SS drag a young man from a group of refugees, put him up against a tree, and shoot him. For hours we wander through woods and fields. My ankle is swollen and my shoe hardly fits anymore. Sometimes, when the path is fairly level or runs down, I sit on the seat of the bike and Herbert pushes me a bit. But mostly I walk.

In the vicinity of Bad Düben on a country road to Eilen-burg, the woman stops near a house slightly set back from the road. "Here it is," she says with a sigh of relief and starts walking toward the driveway with the girls. Herbert and I look puzzled. We didn't know she had a real destination. The woman looks back at us. "Follow me," she beckons.

Herbert looks at me. Helplessly, I point at my foot. A fresh red spot tells me it doesn't look good. For lack of a better plan, we follow the four women to the villa. Just like three days ago at the castle, women and children of high-ranking SS officers have assembled here. A big clock in the kitchen tells us it is two in the afternoon. Tired and hungry, we join the group for a midday snack.

After I have taken off my cap, I see everybody suddenly gazing at me. For a few seconds I have no idea what is going on. Then, to my horror, I see that together with my cap, my turban has come off. The lengthwise shaven strip on my head is revealed. Suddenly there is complete silence. "But those are concentration camp people!" a woman whispers as her eyes almost pop out of their sockets. I calmly drink my coffee and beckon Herbert that it is better to leave.

At the kitchen door, as we look back one more time, the people are still sitting at the table, flabbergasted. I look at the three girls and their mother. They are petrified. I smile briefly, then we leave.

"Let's go in the direction of Eilenburg," I say. "Better not stay around this villa; you never know." Herbert holds the push bike at the rear carrier and pushes me over the road. In the distance there is the sound of gunfire. Apparently, man-to-man combat. Half an hour later, as we are coming out of a stretch of the woods, we suddenly face two soldiers. They approach us with their rifles. Where have I seen those uniforms before?

My memory takes me back to that classroom with soldiers sitting on the floor. The words from back then were just waiting for this one moment to resurface: "Don't worry. It won't be long. It's only a matter of days!" I turn to my companion and exclaim, "We are with the Americans, Herbert! We've made it!"

"German?" the young soldier asks with a clear American accent. "No, certainly not!" I cheer.

Stumbling over my own words, I start to tell them in that wonderful English language that we are survivors of the camps, that on the ninth of April we started to march from Langenstein-Zwieberge with three thousand prisoners, and that we managed to escape but got recaptured. The two Americans listen intently but stay guarded. Only after I have shown them my camp number are they convinced.

They lower their rifles and give us a friendly smile. One of them takes out a pack of cigarettes and offers it to us. These first few minutes are wonderful! No longer in the grip of fear! After a while I ask them if we can continue to the liberated area, and they have to disappoint us. "We are terribly sorry," they say, "but we are not allowed to let anyone through. There is fighting going on everywhere, and we don't have the authority to decide on such matters."

"But you don't expect us to go back?" I ask. They look at each other. "Listen," one of them says, "we won't stand in your way. But remember one thing, you have not seen us or heard from us!" Then they turn back into the woods.

With a sigh of relief, we continue on our way. Within ten minutes we bump into a second American patrol. After we explain who we are, they too tell us they can't let us through. Discouraged, we sit down on the shoulder of the road. "I'm going back," Herbert suddenly says. "I have to get back to my family in Berlin. I don't care." "I am not moving another inch," I say firmly. I roll up the leg of my pants. "Look at this." My foot looks horrible.

The Americans who have listened to our conversation come closer now when they see my wound. They squat down and say, "That does not look good at all. You have to see a doctor immediately." They confer briefly. Then one of them turns around to get help.

Everything moves quickly now. Herbert does not change his mind; he is going to Berlin. With a big hug, we say goodbye. "We'll meet again, after the war," he says with tears in his eyes. He hands me a little piece of paper with his address. "Promise?" I nod with a big lump in my throat. Then he pedals away, his burlap sack strapped to the rear carrier of the bike.

Half an hour later, an American lieutenant in a jeep takes me to Karl Brandt Hospital in Bad Düben, where they put me in a crispy clean hospital ward under snow-white sheets. My burlap sack I put at the end of my bed, within reach.

❖ THE RETURN ❖

Between April 22, when the Americans took me to the hospital, and June 9, the day an ambulance plane took me back to the Netherlands, lies a long story. But I want to make it short. Those last weeks have only marginal significance in my recollection of the camps. A few events from those days, however, are worth mentioning.

My wound recovers perfectly. Within a few days I am able to walk through the entire hospital. Obviously a visit to the central kitchen is not to be missed in those days, and I make sure that I get enough of everything.

A while later I get assigned a beautiful large room that used to belong to the surgeon. When I open the closet, it is full of a variety of clothing. A beautiful gala uniform, all clean and freshly ironed, catches my eye. The surgeon apparently had a high military position. I take the hanger with the uniform out of the closet and hold it in front of me. I get a strong urge that I cannot suppress. I take some clean socks, underwear, shirt, shiny shoes, and the military cap and start to dress.

Minutes later I am staring at a complete metamorphosis in a large mirror inside the door. There stands an arrogant-looking German, chin in the air, straight-backed, cap nonchalantly tilted on his head. I turn around and take a few measured steps through the room. It makes me feel a lot taller and infinitely stronger. Inside me, orders bubble, harsh, metallic words that will force others to move and obey. With my heels clicking, I come to a standstill at the mirror.

I take off my cap. A skinny head with short stubbles of hair on top appears. The image of the arrogant Kraut vanishes, and the look of the victim, the camp prisoner, returns: hollow eyes, still-pale and scurvy skin, powerless. Embarrassed, I put the uniform back in the closet and take out some well-fitting civilian clothes. That superior feeling of my metamorphosis stays with me for a while longer. It is comforting and scary at the same time, but it makes me wonder how fine the line is between torturers and victims. It makes me wonder about man, about me.

Turbulent weeks follow. The Russians are taking over the area between Elbe and Mulde from the Americans, just as the food supplies in the hospital have become critical.

Together with Dr. Veder, a Dutch dentist who is married to a German woman and who works at the hospital in Bad Duben, I go looking for food in the area. In a confiscated white Fiat with red leather upholstery, we scour the countryside. One day we are stopped by Russian soldiers who take our car. A day later, May 9, near a deserted country home, we discover another car, an Adler. It looks all right. We push it out of the barn and try to start it, but to no avail.

At that very moment, a car with four loudly singing Russian soldiers, drunk as can be, passes by. They stop. When they hear we are "Hollanski," they greet us with cheers. We don't immediately understand their exuberance, but finally they manage to explain that last night the Germans unconditionally surrendered to the Russian Supreme Command. The partygoers then start to tow the Adler to Bad Düben. Dr. Veder is ordered to take the wheel. I join the Russians in their car.

It turns out to be a madman's trip. The Adler sails from left to right over the road behind us. Dr. Veder is turning the wheel crazily and is desperately trying to signal that there is something wrong. I try unsuccessfully to convince the Russians to stop. Singing and speaking thickly, they keep going and come to a halt only at the hospital. Veder steps out of the car looking green. He tells me the steering mechanism did not function, and he had been scared to death. Instead of continuing, the Russians get out of the car, and yelling and brandishing their rifles, they disappear in the direction of the hospital.

Later that day we hear that hysterical scenes took place among the nurses. The soldiers apparently lived up to their barbarian reputation concerning women. I realize being in the Russian zone could delay my return home for quite a while.

One day I snatch a motorbike near the hospital and ride it to Eilenburg, about eleven miles south. The Russian commander has his headquarters there. A female guard tells me that evacuees can leave only via Torgau. From there, one is taken to Odessa, in the Ukraine, and from there, eventually, to the south of France.

The prospect of having to travel for weeks or months makes me desperate. I decide to use all my charm and manage to get her to make an appointment with the Russian commander. He can see me that very afternoon.

The man turns out to be a Jewish intellectual from Moscow who welcomes me with open arms. In peacetime he is a professor of French literature at the University of Moscow. Our conversation takes place in French, and he invites me for dinner. During the meal I tell him my entire ordeal.

The commander is deeply touched. He understands all too well how miserable I feel about a trip back home via the Ukraine and southern Europe. He ponders the problem for a while. Then he says, "Why don't you stay with our company a little longer? With your languages and camp experience, you could be of great service with identifying war criminals."

I tell him I am very honored with the offer, but after two and a half years of being a prisoner I really want to go back home. He understands and promises personally to take me to the bridge over the Mulde to hand me over to the Americans tomorrow. And that's what happened.

The weeks following are like a dream. In Delitzsch, I work for a few weeks for Major Moreman as an interpreter in the interrogation of captured German suspects.

A funny thing happens when Dr. Veder and I, with the consent of the major, are taken to Bad Düben in an army Jeep to see if we can pick up the Adler we left at the hospital. Two American soldiers deliver us in the middle of the bridge to Russian guards who take us to the other side. Apparently Russian POWs are using this bridge daily on their return from Germany because suddenly, as we leave the bridge, a band starts to play the Russian national anthem. The moment the officer in charge welcomes us, he realizes that there has been a slight misunderstanding.

Despite a written statement from Moreman, we don't get permission to enter the Russian zone. We return empty-handed to Delitzsch. On our way back on the little country road, we see a young boy in the uniform of the Hitler youth, apparently lost. His eyes are red from crying. Suddenly it reminds me of the third air raid on Monowitz. I see the two crying boys, huddled together and fleeing in deadly fear. They were only kids, just like this boy.

"Stop!" I say to the driver. I ask the boy where he wants to go. He tells me tearfully he is on his way to his mother. He is fifteen years old and has fought in the front line the last weeks. "Everybody has been killed," he cries. "I am the only one of my group who survived."

We take the boy with us to the village where his mother lives and drop him off at his house.

On June 8, I am taken from Bad Düben to Halle in a big army truck. From there, we fly to Welschap near Eindhoven in the Netherlands. The airport is a big distribution center. It is packed with people.

Thousands of people are on their way to all parts of Europe. You can hear a myriad of languages. Some are dressed in the oddest combinations. People in peasants' smocks and uniform pants, people in rags, people still in striped camp attire. With my beautiful tweed coat and expensive shoes that I snatched from the villa at the hospital a few weeks ago, I look rather chic amid this motley group. I almost feel guilty.

After waiting for hours, they announce that the plane that is supposed to take me back home will be delayed until eleven the next morning. In a corner of the departure hall, I, together with hundreds of other people, spend the night under a blanket supplied by the Red Cross. We don't get any sleep at all.

Early in the morning there is another influx of people from everywhere, and soon it is complete chaos. At about nine, an American army truck arrives to distribute food. Thousands of cans of white beans in tomato sauce are delivered. Like starved animals, people gather around the truck.

From a distance, I watch them gobble up their rich meal. Some people have lost all sense of moderation and wolf down two or three cans in a row. Soon they are paying dearly for their gluttony with severe intestinal cramps and diarrhea. I hear that some of them have dropped dead after their overindulgence. I decide not to have any beans; I am not that hungry. The only thing I want is to go home.

At ten-thirty I make my way back through the crowd toward the plane. All of a sudden, amid all the hubbub, I hear somebody call my name: "Louis, Louis!" A bit farther along, a young man enthusiastically waves at me. When I look at him a bit more closely, I recognize Henk van Halst from my hometown of Nijmegen! How is it possible? Henk from high school, Henk with whom I have played soccer, laughed, and drunk! But I am unable to reach him in this stampede. Gesturing powerlessly, I let him know I can't get over to him. "I'll look you up when we're back in Nijmegen," I shout from afar. "Okay," he yells back and keeps waving until I have reached the plane.

With a steady drone, the Dakota makes its way through the patchy clouds. The weather is dull and raining, and we fly at a relatively low altitude. All tucked in, I look out of the little window. At times I can see a glimpse of the gray countryside below us.

I am one of the few of the approximately twenty passengers who are reasonably healthy and who can walk. Most were brought aboard on stretchers. A penetrating smell of disinfectant and tobacco smoke permeates the plane. It makes me feel a bit nauseated. A friendly Red Cross helper wants to know if I am all right. "Yes, all is fine, nothing needed."

Silently I look outside. Eindhoven and then Nijmegen. What will I find there? I am trying to push aside my anxious premonitions about the situation at home, but to no avail. My neck muscles cramp up, and a headache starts to develop. A shock tells me we have landed.

After the plane has come to a standstill, I am the first one to get off. It is still drizzling. So this is the moment I have been longing for with all my soul for the past two and a half years. But there are no cannons firing salutes in the air, no band, no merry flags, no mayor with his chain of office around his neck nervously making a speech.

Somebody directs us to a meadow surrounded by barbed wire. A minute later I am standing in the wet grass in front of a tall man dressed in a uniform of the Verification Service. Two steel blue eyes stare coldly at me. "Anything to declare?" the verifier asks, completely disinterested. For seconds I am speechless. I look at the little bundle of my belongings at my feet. An image emerges. In the snow next to the train lies a marble-white little boy, two red stains slowly spreading over his ripped striped coat. "Anything to declare?" he repeats. "Nothing, only my life," I hear myself answer.

❖ EPILOGUE ❖

On June 10, 1945, Louis arrived in Nijmegen. He found both his sisters alive. Elly and her husband, Paul Vyth, had been in hiding the entire time. Kitty had been deported in September 1944 on one of the last transports from Wester-bork to Theresienstadt and was liberated by the Americans May 11, 1945. Her husband, Leo Kok, died in Ebensee a few days after the war was over.

Only three members of Louis's family survived. His father, mother, Inge, and all uncles, aunts, and cousins were killed.

Louis met his friend Benno once after the war. After Buchenwald, Benno, like Walter Sanders and Elkan Speyer, was liberated after having spent time in a number of other camps in Germany. Benno went home to Belgium.

In 1949, Louis married Netty Huisman. They had six children.

In 1992, Louis, together with a small group of survivors, erected a monument at the site of former camp Westerbork, consisting of 102,000 bricks for each of those who did not return.